Hoover Institutions Publications 101

Peaceful Change
in Modern Society

Contributors

F. Hilary Conroy

Anthony Eden, Earl of Avon

Charles J. Hitch

Sidney Hook

Bernt Ingvaldsen

Bertrand de Jouvenel

Joshua Lederberg

G. Warren Nutter

William G. Pollard

Robert A. Scalapino

Sir Percy Claude Spender

Peaceful Change in Modern Society

Edited with an Introduction by
E. Berkeley Tompkins

The Hoover Institution Press
Stanford University
Stanford, California
1971

The Hoover Institution on War, Revolution and Peace, founded at Stanford University in 1919 by the late President Herbert Hoover, is a center for advanced study and research on public and international affairs in the twentieth century. The views expressed in its publications are entirely those of the authors and do not necessarily reflect the views of the Hoover Institution.

Hoover Institution Publications 101
© 1971 by the Board of Trustees of the Leland Stanford Junior University
All rights reserved
Library of Congress Catalog Card Number: 74-152429
Standard Book Number 8179-1011-6
Printed in the United States of America

To Alicia, Ted, and Ben.
May they grow up in a world at peace.

Contents

Contributors

F. HILARY CONROY is Professor of History at the University of Pennsylvania. He has also taught at the University of California at Berkeley, Swarthmore, and International Christian University in Japan. He has held Fulbright, Social Science Research Council, and Mills fellowships, and has served for many years as the Chairman of the Permanent Conference on Peace Research in History of the American Historical Association. An Asian specialist, he is the author of *The Japanese Frontier in Hawaii* (1953), *The Japanese Seizure of Korea* (1960), *History of Asia* (1964) and *Lessons from Japanese Imperialism* (1967).

ANTHONY EDEN, EARL OF AVON was educated at Eton and Christ Church, Oxford. After military service in World War I, he entered Parliament in 1923 and was a member of the House of Commons until his retirement in 1957, specializing in diplomacy. His long and distinguished career included service as Minister for League of Nations Affairs, 1936; Secretary of State for Dominion Affairs, 1939-40; for War, 1940; and for Foreign Affairs, 1935-38, 1940-45, 1951-55; Deputy Prime Minister, 1951-55; and Prime Minister, 1955-57. His publications include: *Full Circle* (1960), *Facing the Dictators* (1962), *The Reckoning* (1965), and *Towards Peace in Indo-China* (1966).

CHARLES J. HITCH is President of the University of California. A Rhodes Scholar, he has taught economics at Oxford, U.C.L.A., and Berkeley. He served as head of the Economics Division of the Rand Corporation (1948-61) and as Assistent Secretary of Defense (1961-65) before returning to academic life. He is the author of *America's Economic Strength* (1941), *The Economics of Defense in the Nuclear Age* (1960), and *Decision Making for Defense* (1965).

SIDNEY HOOK is Professor of Philosophy at New York University, where he has taught for forty years. He has been a Guggenheim Fellow and President of the American Philosophical Association, and is a Fellow of the American Academy of Arts and Sciences. He is the author of many books, including *The Hero in History* (1943), *Education for Modern Man* (1946), *The Ambiguous Legacy* (1955), *Political Power and Personal Freedom* (1959), and *The Paradoxes of Freedom* (1962).

BERNT INGVALDSEN is President of the Norwegian Parliament and Chairman
of the Nobel Peace Prize Committee. Born in Trondheim, he graduated
from the Norwegian Technical University in 1925. After twenty years as a
successful engineer and business executive, he entered Parliament in 1945.
He was a delegate to the U.N. General Assembly in 1959 and has been
President of the Norwegian Parliament since 1965.

BERTRAND DE JOUVENEL is a professor at the University of Paris. An economist and political philosopher of international renown, he has taught at
leading universities in several nations, including Oxford, Cambridge, Yale,
and Berkeley. An unusually prolific author, his published works include
The Directed Economy (1928), *Towards the United States of Europe*
(1930), *The Reawakening of Europe* (1938), *From One War to Another*
(1941), *On Power* (1945), *America in Europe* (1948), *Ethics of Redistri-
bution* (1951), *On Sovereignty* (1955), and *The Art of Conjecture* (1964).

JOSHUA LEDERBERG, a graduate of Columbia and Yale, is Professor of Biology and Genetics at Stanford University. He is a member of the National
Academy of Sciences and a recipient of the Nobel Prize in Medicine. He
has served on a number of governmental advisory panels in various fields
of science and is also the author of the nationally syndicated column,
"Science and Man."

G. WARREN NUTTER is Assistant Secretary of Defense for International Security Affairs. A graduate of the University of Chicago and an economist by
profession, he has taught at Yale University and the University of Virginia,
where he also served as Director of the Thomas Jefferson Center. He is the
author of *The Extent of Enterprise Monopoly in the United States* (1951),
The Growth of Industrial Production in the Soviet Union (1962), and
articles in various professional journals.

WILLIAM G. POLLARD is Director of Oak Ridge Associated Universities.
Trained as a physicist, he has taught at Rice Institute, the University of
Tennessee, Columbia University, and the University of the South, and has
done advanced research in the field of nuclear physics for the federal
government. He is a Fellow of the American Physical Society and the
American Nuclear Society, and former Vice-Chairman of the Commission
on Peaceful Uses of Atomic Energy. Ordained a priest in the Episcopal
Church in 1954, he has since then divided his efforts between science and

theology. He is the author of *The Hebrew Iliad* (1957), *Chance and Providence* (1958), *Physicist and Christian* (1961), *Atomic Energy and Southern Science* (1966), and *Man on a Spaceship* (1967).

ROBERT A. SCALAPINO is Professor of Political Science at the University of California at Berkeley. He has been a Social Science Research Council Fellow and the recipient of awards from the Rockefeller and Carnegie foundations. He has served as a consultant for the Ford and Rockefeller foundations and the Rand Corporation. He is the author of *Democracy and the Party Movement in Prewar Japan* (1962), *North Korea Today* (1964), and *The Communist Revolution in Asia* (1965), and has contributed to many periodicals and professional journals.

SIR PERCY CLAUDE SPENDER, Australian jurist, diplomat, and statesman, has had a long and distinguished public career, including service as a member of the House of Representatives (1937-51), Minister for the Army (1940-41), Minister for External Affairs (1949-51), Ambassador to the United States (1951-58), Chairman of the Australian Delegation to the United Nations (1952-56), Vice-President of the U.N. General Assembly (1950-51), Australian Governor of the International Monetary Fund (1951-53), Judge (1958-64), and President (1964-67) of the International Court of Justice at The Hague.

E. BERKELEY TOMPKINS, a Senior Fellow at the Hoover Institution and a specialist in the field of American History, served as Chairman of the Institution's Fiftieth Anniversary Conference. He is a graduate of Yale University and the University of Pennsylvania. He has held Harrison, Fels, and Williamsburg fellowships, and has served as Director of the Philadelphia Maritime Museum, Lecturer in the Department of History and Dean of Summer Sessions at Stanford University. He is the author of *Anti-Imperialism in the United States: The Great Debate, 1890-1920*, and his writings have appeared in numerous periodicals and scholarly journals.

Introduction

E. Berkeley Tompkins

Half a century ago Herbert Hoover founded the Hoover Institution on War, Revolution and Peace at his alma mater, Stanford University. Mr. Hoover dedicated the Institution to the study of the causes of war and revolution and to the promotion of peace. In the intervening fifty years the goal of world peace which the great humanitarian sought has unfortunately not been obtained, but rather we have witnessed the most destructive war in all history, as well as numerous lesser conflicts. With the advent of the nuclear age the need for re-analyzing the complex reasons for war and seeking a workable basis for lasting peace has become especially imperative.

Since change is the very hallmark of our era, and since any viable plans for both international and domestic peace must recognize this fact, it seemed appropriate that the conference commemorating the fiftieth anniversary of the founding of the Hoover Instituiton should reflect this salient facet of the modern world in its theme. Peace, if it is based on freedom and is to be enduring, cannot be equated simply with the maintenance of the status quo. There must be an inherent dynamism and flexibility in domestic and international affairs which will allow growth and change to occur in a peaceful and orderly manner.

The conference on Peaceful Change in Modern Society was held over a three-day period in November, 1969, on the Stanford campus. It was partially underwritten by a generous grant from the estate of Thomas Baker Slick, who, like Herbert Hoover, had a strong and abiding philanthropic interest in the cause of permanent peace—a subject on which he published a cogent book in 1958. The conference presentations were grouped under three general headings: (1) War, Peace, and the Nature of Man; (2) Current Threats to Peace; and (3) Paths to Peace in the Future.

In addition to the distinguished statesmen and scholars who authored the papers contained in this volume, the following gentlemen contributed very valuably to the conference by serving as chairmen of sessions and as panelists: Dr. Thomas A. Bailey, Professor of History Emeritus, Stanford University; Dr. Bernard Brodie, Professor of Political Science, University of California at Los

Angeles; Dr. Peter Duignan, Senior Fellow, Hoover Institution; Dr. Harold Fisher, Professor of History Emeritus and former Director of the Hoover Institution; Dr. Samuel P. Huntington, Professor of Government, Harvard University; Mr. Howard P. Jones, former Ambassador to Indonesia and currently a member of the Board of Directors of the *Christian Science Monitor*; Mr. John Owen Lloyd, British Consul-General in San Francisco; and Dr. Richard F. Staar, Associate Director of the Hoover Institution.

Many members of the staff of the Hoover Institution also contributed importantly to the success of the conference, most particularly Mr. Alan Belmont, Dr. Milorad Drachkovitch, Mr. James Hobson, Mrs. Ruth Tobin, and Miss Sarah Uzzell.

The papers presented at the conference and the essays contained in this volume trenchantly examine many of the most significant contemporary questions of peace and peaceful change, setting them in proper historical perspective and offering both sober admonitions for the present and constructive suggestions for the future. The eminent scholars and distinguished statesmen who authored these profound and thought-provoking essays bear eloquent witness to Herbert Hoover's statement that the solution to the problem of peace "must find its origins in human experience and its inspiration in human idealism."

Probably no contemporary statesman has had greater experience in dealing with the problems of peace in the modern world than Anthony Eden, Earl of Avon. His active service in the field of international diplomacy spanned a period of more than three decades. During this time he served with distinction as Foreign Secretary of Great Britain for eleven years and as Prime Minister for the last two years of his public life. Since that time he has remained a keen observer of international developments. In the fascinating lead essay he lucidly reviews past failures and successes in peace-making in the twentieth century, comments cogently on current problems in international relations, and offers some very valuable suggestions for future changes.

Having resigned from the cabinet at a crucial juncture in his career and that of his nation over the question of appeasement, Eden's lengthy discussion of this phenomenon is particularly intriguing. He observes that "it is important to make certain that the consequence of a negotiation is not to gain a little present ease at the expense of more trouble hereafter. Such indulgence becomes all the more blameworthy if the later trouble stored up is at the expense of an ally."

Looking at present as well as past problem areas of the world, Eden focuses his attention on the Middle East and Southeast Asia. He sees solutions in the former area, where again he had enormous personal experience, as basically dependent upon the willingness of the Arab nations to "recognize and accept Israel's continuing existence as an independent state."

Eden was co-chairman (with V. M. Molotov) of the 1954 Geneva Conference on Indochina. He notes that at that time Russia cooperated in settling the conflict there, but that now "unfortunately there is no sign of Moscow's readiness to play a similar part." Nevertheless, he believes that a "solution for Vietnam and all Indochina which each country could accept does exist": the neutralization of the entire area.

Eden sees in the Sino-Soviet conflict another "dangerous international flashpoint." While differences between the major communist powers are viewed with complacency or satisfaction by many Western observers, he believes that this is shortsighted, because "the world is now too constricted for any major upheaval to take place anywhere without far-reaching consequences."

Looking beyond the current areas of tension and conflict to future challenges, Eden perceives the need for a new type of international organization among the nations of the free world. Feeling that the United Nations is too large, diffuse, and unwieldy, and the existing collective security agencies are too confined, he calls for a new organization "among the free nations which would not be geographically limited in scope, but where ideas could be pooled and discussed, and decisions arrived at." This exciting concept comes at a propitious time, when the world is in need of creative new thinking in the field of international relations, and since its enunciation at the conference has already begun to receive widespread consideration. This could be an immensely valuable vehicle for constructive peaceful change, for, as Eden concludes, "if the free nations will make the effort collectively, they can achieve much more than they realize today, not only in their own interest but in the service of this troubled and dislocated world."

There certainly is, and will apparently continue to be for some time, trouble and dislocation in what has in recent years come to be called "the third world." In the volume's second essay, one of the outstanding authorities on the subject, Professor Robert A. Scalapino of the University of California at Berkeley, thoughtfully discusses "World Peace and Revolution in the Third World."

Professor Scalapino, while noting the limitations of the concept, utilizes the term "third world" as a convenient device to describe those non-Western nations which emerged after World War II and which are a part of neither the advanced West nor the Communist bloc. Both individually and collectively these nations are beset by myriad political, economic, social and other problems. Their instability, volatility, and current penchant for seeking change through violent rather than peaceful methods present a grave threat to the peace of the entire world.

Professor Scalapino sees the congeries of difficulties afflicting the third world as basically the result of the trauma which is inherent in the attempt to construct nations out of complex and disparate elements. He astutely analyzes the various cross-currents of racism, tribalism, regionalism, neocolonialism, ethnicity, etc., which further complicate the process, and points out "how the internal pains of nation-building can be exploited for revolutionary purposes by an external force."

Professor Scalapino discusses Nigeria, Biafra, the Sudan, and other problem areas in Africa, where he sees the origins of "continent-wide violence in the future unless solutions can be found." One possible approach here as elsewhere, he notes, would be "to abandon the monolithic concepts of nationalism that have governed so many nation-building experiments in recent years"; and in this regard he urges experimentation with "forms of organization and programs that permit more self-expression at the subnational level." A vital regionalism, together with an effective United Nations in place of the current unfortunately rather moribund organization, could reduce some of the "dangerous potentials" of nationalism and thus provide constructive channels for peaceful change.

Socioeconomic problems in the third world are also detrimental to peace and peaceful change. The population explosion presents the gravest danger. Professor Scalapino feels that control of the earth's rapidly burgeoning population "is as important an undertaking as any single action in the quest for peace in our time." He urges that it receive the highest priority, "for the quality of human life will bear an ever closer correlation to those basic psychological and economic conditions that relate to the overarching questions of peace or war."

The problems of the third world have led to a number of "small wars" which are likely to continue to be the most significant threat to peace in the present era, "especially when these problems are used by other states as a means of seeking to change the regional or global balance of power." It is true that the United States can help to contribute to peaceful change by providing technical and economic assistance to the underdeveloped nations and by helping to maintain a "political equilibrium in the most crucial regions of the world." In the last analysis, however, the relationship between the third world and the broad prospects for peaceful change will depend in large measure on the ability and willingness of the first and second worlds to work together to solve the basic problems and to institute effective multilateral processes of discussion, arbitration, and the enforcement of the tenets of peaceful coexistence.

The next two essays place the fundamental questions facing mankind in philosophical and historical perspective. Professor Hilary Conroy, Chairman of the permanent Conference on Peace Research in History, points out that man has a "natural desire for peace," yet the historical record is replete with examples of strife and warfare. There can be a variety of explanations for this paradox. The eminent French political philosopher Bertrand de Jouvenel, renowned for his brilliant treatises *Du pouvoir* and *De la souveraineté*, concentrates his attention here on the "basic drive for power" in an intriguing and subtle speculative essay.

Professor de Jouvenel states that the principal characteristic of the modern world is the urge "to seek and use ever more power." Above all, ours is "a power-seeking civilization." Professor de Jouvenel views the phenomenon of power in a broad philosophical and historical context. He explores in a free-wheeling manner the full range of its meaning and implications for modern society, and illustrates his fascinating thesis with examples drawn from centuries of history, as well as crucial events as recent as the Czechoslovak rebellion of 1968 and the current Vietnam war.

Hilary Conroy, while acknowledging the reality of the drive for power as well as other "equally unpleasant" realities of the modern world, seeks in the transcendental philosophy of ancient Tibet a clue to the baffling paradox of mankind's difficulty in reconciling his belligerent behavior with his oft-stated desire for peace. Professor Conroy demonstrates through an interesting and perceptive consideration of various facets of both oriental and occidental philosophy, buttressed by historical example, that peace is the goal of rational men. He draws from Tibetan pacifistic thought the belief that if all men "could only see clearly, their compassion would arise out of wisdom and their reliance on violence would cease." The basic message which he thus conveys is the need to educate men for peace. Lasting peace can be obtained and change can be effected in a peaceful manner, but this may necessitate a radical alteration in our way of approaching problems.

G. Warren Nutter, Assistant Secretary of Defense for International Security Affairs, might agree that if all men had obtained the "eye of wisdom" about which Professor Conroy speaks, there would be no need for an elaborate military system. "Men and nations being what they are," however, Dr. Nutter concludes that "there will always be conflicts of interest of all sorts, and the important question is how they will be resolved, whether through coercion or agreement."

Unlike his erstwhile academic colleagues who can deal with the questions of war and peace in a theoretical context, Dr. Nutter must now grapple with these momentous problems in a pragmatic way on a regular basis. He feels that the time unfortunately has not yet come when the United States can realistically decide to unilaterally beat its swords into plowshares.

Like Professor de Jouvenel, Secretary Nutter notes the primacy of the drive for power. He points out that the "leaders of a powerful country determined to have their own way will not be satisfied with resting their case on its intellectual, historical, and ethical merits . . . . They will not shrink from the threat, implicit or explicit, of forcibly denying legitimate rights or of imposing harmful consequences."

Given the realities of such a situation, a nation which wishes to avoid domination and coercion must at present have the means to defend itself adequately. A nation which is, thus, relatively unable to be intimidated by the power of its aggressive adversary can use its power for peace, and the escalating arms race can be scaled down. This is the purpose of the continuing Strategic Arms Limitation Treaty currently being worked out between the United States and the Soviet Union. Each side is aware of the other's power, and therefore less inclined to be reckless and more willing to come to the bargaining table in an attempt to reduce the mutual burden of armaments.

Making a distinction between aggressive and defensive armaments, Secretary

Nutter discusses the merits of the Safeguard system as a deterrent to nuclear aggression, stating his belief that its development is "a move essential for the cause of peace at this historical juncture." If we are safe from potential aggression, we can then work toward building both a stable world order and a better America; if we do not provide for our defense, he soberly warns, "we might have no America to build."

The nuclear weapons described by Secretary Nutter unfortunately form only one part of the deadly and terrifying arsenal which modern man has created. Equally lethal, and perhaps in some ways even more horrifying, are the insidious agents of biological and chemical warfare that have been devised. Nobel Laureate Joshua Lederberg discusses these, analyzes the threat which they pose to mankind, and makes valuable suggestions regarding the redirection of government policy and efforts so that the peaceful application of biological science can be greatly strengthened as an instrument of peaceful change and well-being.

As a brilliant scientist whose own pioneering research has contributed valuable new knowledge for the betterment of the lot of mankind, Lederberg is profoundly disturbed "by the application of this kind of scientific insight to the engineering of biological warfare agents."

Professor Lederberg feels that biological weapons present a graver threat than nuclear weapons. There are several reasons for this. The production of nuclear weapons and vehicles for their effective delivery necessitates the most highly developed industrial technology, with the result that nuclear weaponry has been monopolized by the great powers. He observes that this has been so for a sufficent time "to sustain [as Secretary Nutter also notes] a de facto balance of deterrence and to build a security system based on nonproliferation." Biological weaponry, however, can be inexpensively produced and easily delivered; thus it presents a potential technique of aggression for smaller nations and even for insurgent groups.

Lederberg points out that biological warfare agents "can be expected to be far more capricious than any other form of weapon." They cannot be strategically tested. Their potential destructiveness, while known to be enormous, is incalculable. Their deployment cannot be effectively controlled. Their side effects are unknown. For some newly developed strains of disease which are almost unbelievably lethal, there is no known cure. The possibility of accidental release and resultant epidemics that could wipe out mankind is very real.

For these and other reasons, Lederberg has long argued against any development of biological warfare weapons. In part due to his efforts and the efforts of others of like conviction, President Nixon recently called for U.S. adherence to the Geneva Protocol of 1925 and unilaterally renounced the use of biological weapons. Professor Lederberg applauds this as a valuable initial step, but urges it to be followed as soon as possible by additional action—especially by the immediate implementation of effective international treaty commitments banning forever the use or development of biological warfare agents anywhere in the world.

Whether in the form of biological, nuclear, or conventional weapons, "the sword is not the right weapon for lasting peace," Bernt Ingvaldsen states. Now is the time, the Chairman of the Nobel Peace Prize Committee emphasizes, to› let the sword "remain in the sheath as an antiquated means of solving international questions, and to build harmonious relations between the various countries."

Peaceful coexistence, however, is often a fragile entity. It is an especially difficult proposition, the President of the Norwegian Parliament points out, when some powers, such as the communist nations, are committed to a philosophy of world revolution. While making it quite clear that he feels that the aggressiveness and intransigence of the Soviet Union are prime causes of world tension, Ingvaldsen calls upon all nations to unite in the quest for international understanding and peace. "The responsibility for the destiny of mankind," he states, "rests primarily on the great powers"; to attain lasting peace in the world, "the differences between the great powers must be removed." He feels that a natural economic evolution, with both the communist and capitalist systems gradually moving closer together, will eventually lessen the tensions and antagonisms between the East and West and yield a spirit of greater cooperation and accommodation.

In the international political sphere, the Norwegian statesman urges us to be patient and "elastic" in evaluating the governmental systems of other countries, and to refrain from setting up "too-high barriers between the various shades of democracy." Noting the wide range of extant governmental forms throughout the world, he states that "it does not serve the cause of peace or the interests of any people to demand that our form of government be introduced where it does not fit or where it has no possibility of operating satisfactorily." What the world requires is not any universal form of government, but rather a free and stable system which provides for growth, progress, and peaceful change. He believes that by persistently pursuing the cherished goal of peace, we will ultimately find the power to "elevate life to a higher level and transform the world from militant chaos to a human community."

Two potentially invaluable agents in the transformation process of which Ingvaldsen speaks are international law and organization. Both the problems and the hopes in this sphere are lucidly discussed by the distinguished statesman and jurist Sir Percy Spender of Australia. Mr. Spender, having served both as diplomat and as President of the International Court of Justice, brings a wealth of personal knowledge and experience to the topic which he discusses so forthrightly and skillfully.

Spender's approach to his subject is sober and realistic. He warns that it would be unwise to ignore or attempt to minimize the obstacles that must be surmounted or the problems that must be solved if we are to attain world peace.

He points out that throughout history man's primitive instincts—"instincts of cupidity, acquisitiveness, aggressiveness, assertiveness, pugnacity"—have led to conflict. In the modern era these primordial urges have been channeled into nationalism, that "baleful influence" which, Spender points out, "has limited so much the work of international organizations concerned with peacekeeping, and the efforts of international law to reduce areas of conflict between states and bring order into their relations."

Spender outlines the history and development of modern peacekeeping agencies, beginning with The Hague Convention of 1899, which while not a lasting success, did lay the groundwork for future endeavors in this area. The carnage of World War I further stimulated efforts by thoughtful men to find an organized way to avert future wars, and as a result the League of Nations was created. Unfortunately, the terms of the League Covenant "were imperfect, cumbersome, and crude" and the powers of the Council were "gravely restricted." Nevertheless, even with its drawbacks and disappointing performance in times of international crisis, the League "did represent a very important step forward in man's search for universal peace."

As World War I served as the catalyst for the league, so World War II gave rise to the United Nations. Learning from the mistakes and shortcomings of the League, the authors of the United Nations Charter created a considerably stronger and more efficacious system. The United Nations is better organized and better equipped than the League, and has attempted to do more of a positive nature. The auxiliary agencies of the United Nations (e.g., the World Health Organization, the Food and Agriculture Organization, UNESCO) have done excellent constructive work.

However, the performance of the United Nations' most important entities—the General Assembly and the Security Council—has been less encouraging. In the first decade of its existence the United Nations had a rather "creditable record of peacekeeping." Since then, unfortunately, it has been considerably less effective. Mr. Spender perceptively analyzes the reasons for this. In the Security Council the veto power has been used selfishly and irresponsibly, while the General Assembly has been afflicted by a prevalence of narrow, petty national interests and "the crudity of power politics."

While the United Nations has not lived up to the expectations of its founders, it still remains "the hope of mankind." Spender believes that the United Nations is now in a critical period much like that which the League faced in the mid thirties. Whether it will survive and function successfully as a powerful agency for peace depends on the willingness of its members to "subordinate their individual, separate political interests and national ambitions to the common welfare."

Spender trenchantly analyzes the role and performance of the International Court of Justice on which he served for many years and finds much the same situation there. Although the Court theoretically has a very wide jurisdiction, the submission of cases to it and the acceptance of its decisions are voluntary. He notes various criticisms of the Court, but states that the real difficulty is that the political leaders of too many nations pay lip service to international law but are not really willing to subordinate their power or ambitions to it. International law and international organizations, particularly the United Nations, provide useful vehicles for peaceful change and can "take us, little by little, along the path to a peaceful world," but to do so successfully they need stronger and more genuine support than they have at present.

While Sir Percy Spender is concerned with the threat of international violence, philosopher and historian Sidney Hook, along with a very large segment of the American population, is concerned with the question of violence on the domestic scene. Hook observes that peace among nations and within them fundamentally depends on the "institutional ways of resolving differences of interest." The problem has been approached in a variety of ways and from diverse philosophical positions, not all of them helpful. In fact, as Hook points out, there are "some views about the nature of man and society—some more or less systematically articulated doctrines and attitudes—which make more difficult the achievement of the institutional changes required for peace and peaceful change." Nationalism, which he like Spender distinguishes from patriotism, and racism are two such entities. More threatening to peace and peaceful change, however, is the congeries of disturbing doctrines which Hook terms "the ideologies of violence."

Professor Hook incisively analyzes the theories, strategies, and justifications of violence which are current in America today, points up their fallacies, inconsistencies, and dangers, and offers cogent refutations of both their validity and efficacy.

He dismisses the view advanced in some circles that the entire burden of guilt for violence must rest upon society rather than upon the perpetrators of the violence, and that we must concentrate almost exclusively on the causes of violence and exercise restraint in our condemnation of those who commit it. He points out that we do not always know the causes of violence, that even if we think we do know them it takes time to make necessary adjustments, that violence breeds further violence and that meanwhile it has a dangerously deleterious effect on the "delicate fabric of confidence and trust so essential to a civilized society."

He examines four basic themes of justification for violence in contemporary American society. He finds that these arguments distort historical fact, attempt to justify present evil by citing past instances of it, overlook methods for securing peaceful social change, confuse the role of the state and that of the individual citizen, and reflect a complete lack of faith in the democratic process.

Hook asserts that apologists for violence ignore or obscure the fact that a host of valuable social changes have taken place in this country without recourse to violence or threats of it, and that terror has never been a desirable or effective means of bringing about reform.

Professor Hook warns that violence on the nation's campuses has inflicted a "grievous wound" on the fabric of university life which may take a generation to heal. He sees violence in the academy as an outgrowth of violence in the streets and cities of the country, and concludes that wherever it occurs it damages not only the institution in question but the entire democratic system as well.

Charles Hitch is also much disturbed by the question of violence and disruption on the nation's campuses. In his role as President of the University of California, he has had to confront and deal directly with these distressing phenomena frequently.

In a succinct historical survey of the position of the university in Western society, Dr. Hitch points out that universities have not always been as intimately involved with social change as they are today. In fact, until the mid-nineteenth century their role was viewed as almost exclusively that of repository and transmission agent for the accumulated wisdom of mankind. With the introduction of research in the German universities and the concept of a mission of public service in the American universities, institutions of higher learning became principal agents for change.

Today the university is a focul point of bitter controversy, with diverse groups attempting to enforce ideological conformity. This pressure, from whatever quarter, subverts the principle of academic freedom.

In the past the pressure for conformity came largely from outside the university, but now there is a significant movement for conformity from within the university itself which is "both new and particularly threatening." It has given rise to a distressing and paradoxical situation in which "classrooms are disrupted in the name of education, speakers are shouted down in the name of free speech, job recruiters are driven from the campuses in the name of morality, and demands for total conformity to a particular line of thought are made in the name of nonconformity and dissent." Dr. Hitch condemns these coercive tactics and their specious justification, and calls for a rededication to "freedom of expression and freedom of inquiry, not merely because they sound good as abstract ideals but because they are vital to a healthy university and to a healthy society." What is needed is what Mr. Justice Holmes once called a "free trade in ideas" which allows concepts to be tested "in the competition of the market." In a truly free atmosphere the university can contribute to a valuable "new climate for change" in which we can strive realistically toward our goal of peaceful change in modern society.

The final contributor to the volume, William Pollard, is a man of eclectic talents, who combines the scientific interests of the physicist with the ethical concerns of an ordained clergyman. Both aspects of his professional experience are clearly manifested in the intriguing and thought-provoking essay entitled "Moral Imperatives for Peace in the Remainder of This Century."

A good many of the major problems confronting mankind today, such as the nuclear arms race, racism, and the ideological conflicts between the capitalist and communist worlds, are discussed by other contributors to this volume. While not discounting these disturbing issues and granting their immediate relevance, Pollard suggests that they will soon be superseded by even more basic issues.

"For the first time in history," Pollard states, "men everywhere are beginning to sense that their planet, the earth, is finite, small, and limited in its capacity to support them." The earth's burgeoning population, which is increasing in geometric progression, is placing enormous and potentially insuperable demands on the earth's resources of fresh air and water, food, energy, and basic minerals. Many resources are already in short supply and with the increasing needs caused by the expanding population may within only a few decades reach the point of exhaustion.

Disagreeing with those who predict that further technological advances will solve these problems, Pollard postulates that the industrial-technological revolution of the past two centuries is rapidly coming to an end, and in retrospect from the twenty-first century it will be viewed as "a brief and profligate joy ride—a fleeting instant in the long history of man and his planet."

An appreciable reduction of the rate of population increase will alleviate, but will not eliminate, the basic threat that many vital natural resources may be exhausted. Thus in the future a fundamental ethical and practical problem with strong implications for the peace of the world will be how to apportion the limited resources—"the Commons"—which all mankind must share and utilize, and how to understand and practice a "morality of scarcity."

Pollard cautions that "as we crowd together on the planet, the old bitternesses of race and tribe and nation will become increasingly exacerbated," with the resultant possibility of war. "If warfare does break out over any of the old issues," he notes, "it will be doubly tragic, since these issues are all dying in any event." They will soon be replaced by the pervasive demand for distribution of the remaining reserves of essential resources: "If warfare is to be avoided and peace maintained for the remainder of this century, these are the moral imperatives which must increasingly demand our best thought and action."

The distinguished authors of the papers which follow differ in their background, outlook, and approach, but they are united, as all of mankind must be, in their devotion to peace and the concept of peaceful change.

—1—

Past Failures and Successes in Peacemaking with Suggestions for the Future

Anthony Eden, Earl of Avon

Man is by nature a quarrelsome animal. There have, however, been periods when this troubled planet has enjoyed peace for considerable spells. These have not been very recent. In the age of the Antonines, the civilized world as then known was under the undisputed sway of two enlightened Roman emperors, Marcus Aurelius Antoninus and Antoninus Pius. Except for a few barbaric inroads, Roman control was absolute.

It was two thousand years before Europe enjoyed any comparable period of peace, and that was disturbed by internal ferment. It remains true, however, that the Congress of Vienna did a good job after the fall of Napoleon. For forty years between the Battle of Waterloo in 1815 and the Crimean War the peace of Europe was unshattered; and for the hundred years until 1914 wars, though sharp and bloody, as the Franco-Prussian War and the American Civil War, were not global or even continental.

It is worth considering why the Congress of Vienna was so comparatively successful. In part this was due to the statesmanship of two remarkable men, Lord Castlereagh for England and Prince Metternich for Austria. But this was not the whole story. The victorious alliance which included Prussia and Russia had no desire to humiliate the enemy, France. On the contrary, Napoleon having been eliminated, the victors accepted the need for a reconstructed France who could play her part in Europe.

After the holocaust of the First World War, statesmen attempted once again to rebuild at Versailles. This treaty has been much criticized, at times I think unfairly. There was certainly nothing reprehensible in the attempt to create a League of Nations, and its Covenant was well drafted. In the heyday of its power, the League of Nations commanded an authority which was well deserved. These years immediately following the signing of the Treaty of Locarno brought Germany back into the comity of nations with Britain, France, Italy, and the Low Countries.

The most important feature of the League at that time was the quarterly meeting of the Council. This body, composed of about eleven members,

12

included the representatives of the leading European powers as well as of South America, the Little Entente, Asia, and one of the British Dominions. The foreign secretaries of the principal European powers almost invariably attended in person, and the other member states were represented by leading nationals.

As a result, the Council's debates were of high quality and its meetings, which usually lasted about a week, were most useful occasions for joint and several discussions between the foreign secretaries. In 1926, the first occasion on which I attended one of these meetings as Parliamentary Private Secretary to Sir Austen Chamberlain, I was present at a number of conversations between Sir Austen; the French Foreign Secretary, Monsieur Briand; and the German Foreign Secretary, Herr Stresemann. Their discussions were often quite informal and no doubt the mutual confidence built up between these three men promoted easier relations for Europe during those years.

On the other hand, the League of Nations suffered from certain shortcomings, which were to prove fatal. The gravest of these was its limited membership. Unhappily President Wilson had not been able to guarantee United States membership; added to this, Soviet Russia did not become a member until 1935, after Germany's withdrawal. As a result the League was not strong enough to deal with the Manchurian crisis, nor were its material resources sufficient to ensure the success of the sanctions policy against Mussolini four years later. Even had there been a sufficiently firm collective will in both instances it has to be remembered that in international affairs resources beget confidence.

Another controversy of these years between the wars concerned the much debated term "appeasement." There was no harm in the original use of that word, which could be translated as an attempt to reduce the international temperature and thereby promote peace, but now it also carries a pejorative meaning. While attempts at negotiations in themselves are not to be condemned, it is important to make certain that the consequence of a negotiation is not to gain a little present ease at the expense of more trouble hereafter. Such indulgence becomes all the more blameworthy if the later trouble thus stored up is at the expense of an ally; and it is often found that the time said to have been gained turns out to have benefited the potential aggressor.

Therefore, I would say that while it was not wrong to attempt negotiations with Hitler and Mussolini, it was certainly wrong to place uncritical confidence in their assurances. On one occasion in particular, during the Spanish Civil War, the democratic powers were able to show firmness and the consequences were salutary. During August 1937 attacks on merchant ships were taking place in increasing numbers in the Mediterranean. Most of these attacks were by submarines, and at the end of the month a British destroyer was unsuccessfully attacked in this way sixty miles south of Valencia. In theory these submarines were Spanish. In fact their number was much too large for this to be possible, and, as the weeks passed, we had increasing evidence that on Mussolini's orders about fifty Italian submarines were attacking ships in the Mediterranean. The purpose was to blockade Valencia and Barcelona, but the consequence was to sink the shipping of a number of nations sailing on lawful occasions.

The British and French governments decided that this situation could not be tolerated, and agreed to call a conference of the Mediterranean powers at Nyon, Switzerland (September 10-14, 1937), to formulate plans to patrol the Mediterranean. We realized that the main burden of this exercise must fall on our two countries, but we hoped to receive useful support from the conference, which after some hesitation Mussolini decided not to attend.

Our plan was that our naval patrols would have orders to fire on any submarine attacking a non-Spanish ship, it being agreed that none of the submarines of the Nyon powers would put to sea in the Mediterranean unless accompanied by a surface vessel. In order to make these patrols effective beyond doubt, the Royal Navy supplied thirty-five destroyers and the French twenty-eight.

The Conference at Nyon reached agreement on these proposals. Mussolini was informed and allotted an area including the Tyrrhenian Sea which he could patrol if he wished and, as I was to write later, "This was done in order to offer a large area, as befitted Fascist dignity, to Mussolini, who could then send his warships to hunt his own submarines where it mattered least. We did not expect that Italy would accept this offer outright, but it could form the basis of a bargain, and our position was strong."

In the event, the instructions given to the allied navies at Nyon were completely successful. No Italian submarine showed itself from that day and piracy in the Mediterranean, in that form at least, came to an end. It was not the least advantage of the Nyon Conference that it was over in forty-eight hours, with its agreements reached and its action set on foot. The support of the smaller powers including Yugoslavia, Greece, and Turkey was significant and helpful. We were thus able together to patrol the main Mediterranean trade routes from Suez to Gibraltar, from the Dardanelles to Gibraltar, and from the North African ports to Marseilles.

This action, of course, was possible because Anglo-French naval power was overwhelming in the Mediterranean. A difficulty for the diplomacy of our two countries in the thirties was that we rarely had the chance to act in such conditions of strength. However, even though such opportunities were difficult to find, it was diplomacy's job to seek them out.

Unfortunate examples of appeasement were not confined to the interwar years. In the late fifties and the early years of this decade, pressure was put on the Netherlands to abandon its sovereignty over Western New Guinea. The Indonesian dictator, Sukarno, confiscated Dutch property and Dutch shipping trade between the islands. Compensation, the Indonesian government declared, would be paid only when the Netherlands abandoned Western New Guinea. Sukarno's claim to that territory had no ethical or ethnical justification, but it succeeded under pressure from the United Nations, apparently in the hope that this concession would appease a greedy appetite. As should have been foreseen, this optimism was unjustified. Appetite grew and Sukarno was soon mounting demands against Malaysia. This was euphemistically called "confrontation." The aggression was resisted but at the cost, inevitably, of lives on both sides and of some impoverishment of Indonesia.

It would have been much better for everyone concerned, especially Indonesia and her people, if Sukarno's earlier demand and depredations had not been condoned and encouraged.

It seems clear, therefore, what the statesman's position on this question of appeasement should be. There is no need to adopt an inflexible attitude of refusal to discuss differences with powers with whom we disagree, unless by so doing we weaken an ally or encourage the appetite of a potential aggressor. Special prudence in this respect is necessary when dealing with a militant dictatorship, which imposes censorship at home and indulges ambitions abroad.

It has indeed to be admitted that, to a limited but serious degree, a democracy can be at a disadvantage in a diplomatic engagement with a dictatorship. The hide of censorship and skillful state-directed propaganda are not easy to penetrate or counter. In a free community a minister can always expect generous doses of advice from friends and critics alike on how to play his hand, while a dictator can play his cards close to his chest. Despite these disadvantages, we would not have it otherwise, for a democracy draws strength from its freedom of thought and criticism while a dictatorship can suffer deep cracks in its fabric which, though hard to discern, may prove fatal.

*   *   *

The League of Nations differed in another important respect from our own present-day practice. The Covenant of the League was associated with the peace treaties which brought the First World War to an end. Some thought this a weakness, creating a certain rigidity in League thinking, but another side to that contention was the instinct of the League, as well as its obligation, to uphold existing treaties. There was only one exception: any international obligation could be modified by agreement of the parties to it. Apart from this, commitments once entered into had to be respected. The Council of the League admittedly included a number of countries with a vested interest in the peace treaties—among others, France, Czechoslovakia, Rumania, Yugoslavia, and to a modified extent the United Kingdom, Belgium, and the British Commonwealth. It was not, however, entirely harmful for any country, including those pressing for a revision of existing treaties, that there should be this predilection for upholding existing obligations. It has to be recognized that such a tendency strengthens international law and upholds the standards which are indispensable for international confidence.

Today the greatest peril resides in a failure to respect treaties or uphold obligations. Almost any pretext is thought to be good enough to justify a violation of a hitherto accepted rule or treaty. This is a dangerous indulgence and it is spreading widely. The hijacking of aircraft, the seizing and imprisonment of passengers engaged on their lawful business, the planting of bombs in defiance of armistice agreements even in countries far removed from the conflict but chosen for their alleged sympathies, these are all nefarious practices and must be stamped out if the world is not to drift to anarchy, which would cost every nation dear but press hardest on the poorest.

There could be no more cynical commentary on the contempt in which international obligations are now held than the recent action of the Syrian government, which released the hijackers of an American commercial airplane, who had forced it to land at Damascus while retaining in captivity two civilian passengers who had been lawfully traveling on the same aircraft. If behavior of that kind is internationally tolerated, we are well set on the road to anarchy.

It is probably still true that the dread of the nuclear deterrent is such that the dangers of conflict between major powers are less than they were in the early years of this century. On the other hand the growing habit of a number of countries to take the law into their own hands on issues of international concern will, if unchecked, weaken international confidence to a point where it can undermine the welfare of all nations.

There is also an inevitable spread of nuclear knowledge. So far, two countries with important practical know-how, France and China, have shown no readiness to sign any arms agreement covering nuclear weapons. It may be that the French government will in time modify its attitude; China is more problematical and potentially a cause for graver concern.

Apart from this, there is also the danger of the spread of nuclear weapons, which can only be countered by international agreement and only be effective if universally applied. We are far from either of these conditions today.

In spite of an anxious Middle Eastern situation, we should not avert our eyes from another dangerous international flashpoint at this time, the Russo-Chinese relationship; this despite a recent meeting between Premier Kosygin and Premier Chou En-lai. In the short view it could be argued that differences between two leading communist powers should be regarded with complacency or even satisfaction by the free world. This would be a mistake because the world is now too constricted for any major upheaval to take place anywhere without far-reaching consequences. We stand to gain by some adjustment of Russo-Chinese differences but it is not going to be easy to arrive at, for the roots of disagreement strike deep.

China is obsessed by the memory of what she regards as Russian territorial conquests, purloined in tsarist days. Moreover China needs room and raw materials, which is why I have never been convinced that Peking has any deep ambition to conquer Indochina. A friendly, or at least neutral, neighbor to the south would be welcome, but there would be little wisdom in a Chinese attempt to establish direct rule over a thickly populated country in any part of the world. A controversy on the Chinese-Russian border is in another and graver context.

*   *   *

It is impossible to survey the world scene without being conscious of its growing disarray. The United Nations will do what it can, but its capacities are limited. The authority of the Security Council has suffered by over-indulgence in the use of the veto by the communist powers and that of the Assembly, to some extent, by the multiplicity of its membership.

The free world has set up a number of organizations to deal with dangerous points around the earth's surface. Three of these are of international signifi-cance: NATO, SEATO, and CENTO. The most important of these is NATO, now in some danger of falling a victim to its own success because it has provided a firm shield to protect Western Europe, which has lived of recent years snugly, if not smugly, behind it.

There is a disposition to suggest that the world can do without NATO. That would be a profound error. The shield is still needed but it should be possible for NATO to take on certain further responsibilities. It could become a diplomatic instrument for negotiation with the Warsaw powers. Collective negotiation on this basis between the countries on either side of the iron curtain could one day be useful. You may ask, "What kind of thing can they discuss?" I would reply with the experience of years gone by.

At the Summit Conference at Geneva during the summer of 1955 each of the Western governments put forward suggestions for discussion. None of them made any notable progress at the time. However, a suggestion I made, that we should consider the creation of a demilitarized zone on either side of the iron curtain and an agreed withdrawal of forces on either side of the zone, was taken up later by the Russians. Bulganin made reference to it in a note made public in April 1957, and declared his government's readiness to discuss it, together with some other proposals which could have been helpful. Unfortunately, the Secre-tary of State for the United States at that time turned down this suggestion.

I mention this because, in my experience, it sometimes happens that pro-posals put forward at one international forum can come to fruition years later in another setting. The opportunity could certainly arise when Europe could find use for this and comparable suggestions to its own advantage.

The Middle Eastern crisis is still with us. It is in more dangerous shape now on account of the failure to make a true diagnosis or apply an instant remedy at an earlier date. There has been too much wishful thinking, always a tempting indul-gence for democracies.

Yet the heart of the matter is unchanged. Peace in the Middle East, as else-where, depends on the observance of treaties and obligations. It also depends upon the willingness of Israel's neighbors to recognize and accept that country's continuing existence as an independent state. It may seem strange to have to say this so many years after the principal powers of the world have recognized Israel as a soverign state; Soviet Russia was indeed one of the first to do this. To call a halt to repeated attempts to destroy the state of Israel is the prime condition of peace, after which all other difficulties, such as territorial questions and the settlement of Arab refugees, are, I am sure, soluble.

The world has a responsibility in this business also. It was not, after all, Israel which provoked the events of 1967. It was not Israel which closed the Gulf of Aqaba, or marshalled its armor in the Sinai Peninsula, or threatened the annihila-tion of a neighbor. Yet having endured these menaces and acted at the last moment for her own salvation, it is hardly surprising that Israel should want to see some prospect of a permanent settlement as a counterpart to any contri-bution she could make.

I am convinced that once recognition of Israel is granted by its neighbors, as it is already by the rest of the world, negotiations, though arduous, can make progress.

The four powers may be able to help but eventually an intermediary, like Ambassador Jarring, will be needed to facilitate direct contacts if peace is to be made. The tragic part of this whole business is that there is no limit to the prosperity the area could enjoy if settlement could once be reached. Just give the bitterness a chance to die and confidence a chance to grow and the outcome could surprise the most bigoted and the most cynical.

* * *

Washington and Moscow are seeking openings for negotiations. Nuclear wea-pons evidently come first and it is welcome news that a start is being made with these. There is also talk of a package deal between the two superpowers. That may not be the best way to proceed. It could be too ambitious, and I think it would be wiser to work at the package deal item by item. It would be good if Vietnam could be placed high on the list.

There is no doubt that Russia played a constructive part in negotiating the 1954 agreements at Geneva which ended the French Indochina war. I can bear testimony to that. Mr. Molotov and I were co-chairmen of the Geneva Confer-ence and I do not think we could have got through without his help. Unfortu-nately, there is no sign of Moscow's readiness to play a similar part now. Yet the solution for Vietnam and all Indochina which each country could accept does exist. It is the neutralization of the area.

North Vietnam does not want to be dominated by China or Russia. The United States wants to get out of South Vietnam. Laos and Cambodia want to be left alone to manage their affairs free from North Vietnamese inroads. These are the ingredients of a settlement, if Hanoi does not make the mistake of thinking it can have everything its own way in the expectation that American opinion will force the government to abandon the South. That could prove a dangerous illusion. Hanoi may overcall its hand.

North and South must decide what their mutual relationship should be, but that is scarcely possible yet. The immediate need is for the South to decide what its own future shall be, and it has a right to be allowed to do this free from Northern intervention. For instance, it is not acceptable that Hanoi should seek to dictate the composition of the government of South Vietnam, any more than South Vietnam would be justified in formulating similar demands against the North.

It should cause no surprise if the time for any final arrangement in Indochina has to be measured in years rather than in months. Laos and Cambodia are unlikely to want the same kind of government as North Vietnam, and almost certainly South Vietnam will want something different, but as neutralized countries they could all grow to understand the advantage they get from their neutrality, not only in politics but in commerce and trade too. There are, for instance, enormous possibilities in the development of the Mekong Delta which is just the job for the World Bank. Once the fighting has stopped.

* * *

As we conclude this survey, I should like to consider whether there are any further practical arrangements the free world can make for joint consultation and action to its collective advantage. Present methods are hardly ideal and could evidently be improved upon. There are frequent visits two and two, mostly to Washington, and there are the regular meetings of such allied organizations as NATO. Yet for the most part these are patchy, in the sense that they cannot cover the interests of the free world as a whole. The free nations need to coordinate their political and economic policies more closely. This is especially true if they are to have their maximum influence, as we must surely desire.

It is not possible to carry through this work in the United Nations, nor is NATO large enough in the area it covers. I would like to see consideration given to some organization among the free nations which would not be geographically limited in scope, but where ideas could be pooled and discussed, and decisions arrived at. The secretariat of such an organization need not be elaborate, but the outcome of its efforts could be useful and constructive.

It is, of course, true that the power of the United States far exceeds that of

any other single nation in the free world. In that sense such an organization could be regarded as superfluous. On the other hand, it is to the advantage of even the most powerful nation to take counsel from time to time with its friends, especially since it is lonely at the top.

Such an organization as I have suggested need not conflict in any way with the United Nations any more than NATO does. On the contrary, insofar as it facilitates coordination of policies in the free world it must be an influence for good. In these days the improvement in communications, the invention of new media, and the attendant publicity of television jostle the old-fashioned methods of diplomacy, sound as these were. We need a form of machinery which will facilitate the exchange of thoughts and policies between the free nations. The world has now become too small for issues to be settled only within continents.

This at least is certain: each of the free nations has responsibilities which it must be prepared to discharge if it is to preserve the way of life in which it believes. There cannot be for any one of us any refuge in isolation. If we were to indulge such false hopes, you with your great responsibilities and we with our lesser ones, we would only be increasing the dangers of a third world war. Our course must be the opposite: to work out together what each can do.

If the free nations will make the effort collectively, they can achieve much more than they realize today, not only in their own interest but in the service of this troubled and dislocated world.

—2—

World Peace and Revolution in the Third World

Robert A. Scalapino

Let me begin with a confession. In several senses, my topic is a misnomer. One can argue legitimately that there is no third world, just as there are no first or second worlds. And even if one accepts, as a convenience, the concept of a third world, serious questions can be raised as to whether this world is truly involved in a revolution at present.

Generally, the term "third world" is used to describe those non-Western societies which became political entities after World War II, and which belonged neither to the advanced West nor to the communist bloc. Thus, the term was and is a political one, used in juxtaposition to the supposed first and second worlds, namely the West and the Communists. For most purposes, however, the real world is not divided into three component parts, politically or otherwise. Both the divisions and the unions are infinitely more complex. Major differences in culture, resources, and institutions within the third world are at least as important as the basic problems they share. This is repeatedly illustrated in the thought and the actions of the new states. It is abundantly clear, moreover, that the first and second worlds are currently subject to numerous centrifugal tendencies, and that they too have a limited reality at most.

Equally germane is the question of revolution and its relation to the third world. The term "revolution" is at once a useful and an imprecise term, applied in many ways for many purposes. If by revolution one means a fundamental change in the character of the society, encompassing socioeconomic as well as political values and institutions and produced either peacefully or through violence, then the most revolutionary society of our times is the United States. The tempo of the American revolution is more rapid, and the thrust into all segments of this society deeper than is true of any of the third world (or communist) revolutions. For the most part, change in the third world, even when it is relatively swift, still has its major impact upon a small elite. The great bulk of the people continue to live, think, and act in a relatively traditionalist manner— even though traditionalism can often be used on behalf of new causes and new men. Indeed, one of the destabilizing factors in these societies is the widening

21

gap between elites and masses, a gap which throws into question both the legitimacy and the authority of many governments irrespective of their precise character.

The above strictures must be kept in mind as we explore the complex problems involved in the relation between third world developments and global peace. Now let us turn to the problems themselves, beginning with nationalism and the nation-state, issues close to the heart of contemporary politics. First the West and now the world have accepted the nation-state as the most appropriate political unit around which to focus mass loyalties in our times. The nation was not always regarded as the ideal political unit, it must be emphasized, and it may not be eternally so. Indeed, both the integrity and the worth of the nation-state are under severe challenge today, in the advanced as well as in the developing societies, and as a concept it is being attacked from diverse quarters, the charges being both that it is too small and too large. Many of modern man's problems go beyond the capacity of the nation, it is alleged, even as it is argued that many of his psychic needs can only be met by smaller political units. We live in an age when the most basic issues of political organization and ideology are being reraised.

It is thus an extremely difficult time in which to engage in nation-building. A century ago, a society was allowed more leisure and more isolation as it proceeded with this complex task. Today, isolation—except for the highly authoritarian society—is very difficult, and leisureliness almost impossible. The goal is often that of a one-generation revolution. But instant nationhood, like instant development, is a myth. Despite the roster of the United Nations, there are very few genuine nations in the world today, and the trauma involved in trying to build nations is one of the principal threats to peace at present.

In most societies, particularly those of the third world, tribalism, regionalism, and ethnic divisions are intense. These are not new phenomena, of course, but the very process of seeking to subordinate them to the requirements of a modern nation has in many cases intensified them. Colonialism depoliticized the people, because the colonial system was not served by mass mobilization, especially in political terms. Even in noncolonial settings, however, efforts to politicize the people have increased greatly in scope and sophistication in very recent times. But often the effort to create nationalist sentiment quickly has resulted, paradoxically, in an increased consciousness of separate group identities. Racism, ethnicity, and tribal-regional bonds, all in a variety of forms, have never been more vital a part of the political scene throughout the world than they are today.

Is this a threat to peace? The answer is clearly yes, although one must distinguish between the threats of local, regional, and more massive conflicts. There are many parts of the world today where local or regional conflicts of a racial or ethnic character have taken a heavy toll of lives. Witness only the most recent struggles in such societies as the Sudan and Nigeria, or the earlier conflicts in India, the Congo, and Indonesia. It is apparent also that ethnic factors, combined with religious and other issues, hang heavily over the Israel-Arab crisis. Certainly, these divisions, in the Middle East and elsewhere, constitute a major threat to peace on regional and even global bases.

Consider, for example, the immediate tensions involved throughout South and Southeast Asia where violence based upon subnational groups lies always just beneath the surface and frequently erupts into the open. It was once assumed that racial tensions in Asia revolved primarily around the white man's presence and that the end of colonialism would witness a decline in such problems. This has proved to be totally untrue. And whether racial-ethnic conflicts can be contained within a given state depends in considerable part upon the interests of other states in the immediate vicinity in either abetting the conflict or dampening it down. For example, racial-ethnic-tribal troubles in South and Southeast Asia have especially ominous connotations at present because both the Chinese and the North Vietnamese communists are actively supporting a number of challenges to the established national regimes by such groups. The training and military equipment given to such dissidents as the Naga of Assam, the Kachin and Karen of Burma, the Meo and other hill peoples of Thailand, Laos, and Cambodia are graphic examples of how the internal pains of nation-building can be exploited for revolutionary purposes by an external force. How successful such exploitation can be is, of course, another question.

In Africa, also, with different issues at stake and to a different degree, racial crises promise continent-wide violence in the future unless solutions can be found. Only the relative failures of development within Black Africa to date have prevented major assaults upon White Africa in which Freedom Fighters trained, armed, and equipped externally would seek the "liberation" of states under white rule. On a small scale, these movements go on nevertheless, despite multiple problems and cleavages—personal, ideological, and organizational— among the revolutionary forces.

Once again, the degree of external commitment to such movements can make a substantial difference. One can contrast the various national liberation movements directed against Mozambique, Rhodesia, and the Republic of South Africa— or the earlier Congo rebellion—with the case of the Sudan. Unquestionably there was unhappiness in countries like Uganda over the massacre of southern blacks by northern Sudanese, and refugees in substantial numbers were accepted, but no intervention, either direct or indirect, was contemplated. Hence, conflict here was "contained" within the Sudan despite the significant proportions it reached.

The Nigeria-Biafra crisis was somewhat different. Here, both parties to a civil war received external assistance, although foreign troops were not injected. Indeed, Biafra represented one of those issues with international ideological-political connotations. Nigeria, to some, represented the perfidy of British colonialism combined with the iniquities of major-power intervention in a post-colonial era—intervention, that is, on behalf of a "corrupt, repressive" government. This indictment, moreover, was leveled against the Soviet Union as well as the West, since at least nominal support for Nigeria came from these quarters. Biafra, for many "movement" people, was a symbol of the struggle against oppression, even genocide, and perhaps more importantly was also a symbol of the righteousness of smallness against the evils of bigness. When Biafra won the support of Tanzania in Africa, and of the Chinese People's Republic, its anti-establishment symbolism was confirmed.

Thus Biafra, along with many other events in the third world, illustrates how that world can become quickly involved in the politics of the first and second worlds, and how difficult it is in our time to maintain the boundaries of national and international politics.

Even a small number of people who regard such boundaries as meaningless or evil can have a pronounced impact within their nation if organizational and media facilities are available to them. At the very least, this adds new dimensions to the political conflict in a wide range of societies throughout the world. The fact that Biafra—not to mention Vietnam—can beome an integral part of political conflict in many parts of the world, including the type of internal conflict involving violence, indicates the complex nature of our time and suggests one of the many reasons why isolation for a major world power is virtually impossible in the late twentieth century. Most third world disputes will find their way into American thought and life, including American political processes, even if American forces are not involved. And if major trends of a disintegrative nature develop in the third world, they will affect the entire character of American political life.

The thrust of these remarks is to signal the fact that racial and ethnic issues will loom large in the politics of the future, and pose a major threat to peace, both domestic and international, in the years ahead. The threat will not be less for the first and second worlds, as we know only too well. Racial problems in any society tear at the fabric of loyalty and cause some individuals or groups to commit themselves to foreign causes and states as a supreme sign of alienation. Let it be reiterated that white versus nonwhite conflict is only one element in the scene. It figures prominently in the United States, it is one vital factor (but only one) in the racial turmoil in Africa, and it is a factor also in the Sino-Soviet struggle. When one looks at the total international scene, however, the conflicts based upon race, ethnic group, or tribe are vastly more complex and frequently do not involve whites at all.

If these conflicts are a danger to peace, can this danger be reduced? Clearly there is a great need today to abandon the monolithic concepts of nationalism that have governed so many nation-building experiments in recent years, and to experiment with forms of organization and programs that permit more self-expression at the subnational level. Monolithism in all forms is undemocratic, but perhaps more important it is unworkable in the end, whatever the degree of coercion applied. Unfortunately, a double standard is currently being applied by many representatives of the third world in this respect. They rigorously criticize the policies of white supremacy being pursued in such states as Rhodesia (and their criticism is often just, in my opinion), but their public silence on events in the Sudan or Burma, to take but two examples, is deafening.

If an internal attack upon this problem is important both to domestic and international peace, there is an equally essential step concerning which we shall have more to say later, namely the need to define the requirements of peaceful coexistence, and to establish some international system of patrolling these requirements. There can be no peace in our time unless we accept the fact that external intervention in the internal affairs of another society is by far the most common means of interstate conflict today, especially as it applies to the third world, and that this problem requires attention from the international community now.

The current racial and ethnic fissures being displayed so prominently in the third world, however, are only one side of the coin. If the nationalist movement is predominantly an elitist movement in emerging states, and one hinged to a cult of personality in many cases, it is still the most powerful political movement currently operative. Some observers, while condemning most manifestations of nationalism in advanced nations like the United States, are prepared to encourage nationalism indiscriminately in the second and third worlds. They overlook the fact that while nationalism is both necessary and inevitable at this stage of man's political development (and in *all* parts of the world, including the United States), it can also be a dangerous force if misused.

Indeed, the past century is replete with examples of nationalism run wild, producing massive conflict in the end. It is by no means clear that the third world (or the second world) will escape the pitfalls of virulent nationalism filled with antiforeignism, the mythology of racial supremacy, and an insistence upon some type of expansionism as a sacred duty. Revolutionary literature coming out of the third world today often combines the gospel of hatred with a vigorous defense of violence. Conflict, indeed, is rationalized and defended in terms scarcely distinguishable from those used by Hitler or Mussolini. War is legitimatized as the only possible means of remedying grievances and advancing truth.

Sukarno in his day illustrated well the dubious uses to which nationalism could be put in a new Asian state. Even in the Philippines, a prototype of an excolonial society that has managed to preserve democratic political institutions, the use of nationalism in a highly irrational fashion was recently demonstrated in connection with Sabah. Nation-building, with its need for cohesive, unifying forces, provides the temptation to create issues out of non-issues, to use external enemies as a substitute for a serious tackling of internal problems.

In sum, there is a real threat that the mistakes associated with nation-building in the past will be repeated by the states now emerging, including those attitudes and actions that led to numerous conflicts in the course of the last several centuries. If they are repeated, moreover, they will be repeated in an era markedly different—one in which the weapons of destruction, even for small states, are infinitely more powerful and in which the boundaries between localized and international conflict are far more difficult to maintain. Thus, despite the challenges mounted against it, nationalism will remain one of the powerful forces of our time and one of the most dangerous, capable of being used for many purposes, constructive and destructive, but always containing a sizable quotient of irrationality.

Once again, it is not sufficient merely to define the problem if we are concerned about peace. What can be done? At the outset, certain admissions of failure or weakness should be made. None of the regional or international political instruments currently at our disposal are operating effectively. The prestige of the United Nations has never been so low, and its performance has never been so disappointing. With a few exceptions, moveover, the same assessment could be made of regional organizations. In East Africa, for example, the plans for federation have been almost completely abandoned. In West Africa also, regionalism is at a low ebb. One scarcely needs to be reminded of the problems that have attended inter-American organizational efforts; even in Asia, where the need for regionalism is most acute; groups like ASEAN and ASPAC face an uncertain future.

Effective regionalism and a meaningful United Nations represent one means, perhaps the only available means, of counterbalancing nationalism and reducing some of its dangerous potentials. This is a time when our creative energies should be directed as never before toward making regional organizations—economic, social, and political as well as military—perform the functions for which they were intended, and which are so desperately needed. Is there a better time than now, moreover, as we approach the twenty-fifth anniversary of the founding of the United Nations, to reexamine thoroughly the Charter of that body, its structure and performance, prepared to make major changes that may breathe life into a body that is perilously close to death, albeit a lingering death?

There is a special need for such activities because of a giant paradox which increasingly marks our time: in a period when a myriad of new states are trying to emerge simultaneously into the world-stream, most of them beset with difficulties far beyond their capacity to tackle unaided, certain of the most "advanced" societies are threatening to enter a withdrawal phase as a result of having to face a host of new internal problems that have accompanied the most recent stages of modernization. In sum, the revolution now sweeping over nations like the United States may produce such a drastic reordering of priorities as to return this nation to a quasi-isolationist stance, permitting the problems of international development and order to gather momentum until once again global conflict is at hand. This indeed is the central issue of our time, and unless it is faced squarely, solutions to lesser problems will be to little avail. Only through effective regional groupings, where responsibilities are shared, and only via a drastically altered United Nations, where role and capacity are more closely interrelated, can the issues at hand be realistically approached.

Meanwhile, what threats to peace are posed by socioeconomic conditions in the third world? Certain trends are easily projected in the direction of tragedy. None is more frightening than the population explosion that has taken place in the past century. With pestilence increasingly controlled and nuclear war a more remote possibility, will population growth in certain areas, mainly in the third world, advance to the farthest reaches of the food supply and beyond? We are told that today's population of approximately 3.5 billion will reach 4 billion by 1975, and possibly 7 billion by the end of this century.

The most serious aspect of this population explosion may not be the purely economic one. It is entirely possible that if population increases can be kept within the above range, our capacity to provide food and shelter will generally suffice in an age of remarkable scientific-technological advances. At most, the truly acute economic problems may be confined to certain pockets, regions where the population-resource ratio is worse. But will human organizational skills and the human psyche be able to cope with massive increases in population density and the remorseless pressure of individuals, one upon another, without relief?

There is a growing body of evidence that the strains of congestion bear directly upon the political value and institutions of a society, and indeed, upon all aspects of human life. The total disappearance of privacy from life might quite possibly have even graver political than economic consequences. Does not the potential for violence—and for authoritarianism—greatly increase if masses of people are constantly rubbing up against one another, living in huge conglomerates? Can one, under such circumstances, attain or keep a respect for the value of human life, a concern for human dignity—the type of values, in sum, that are helpful in causing mankind to accept peaceful approaches to change? Or is man, at the height of his glory and in the midst of the most extraordinary technological revolution, doomed to descend toward the animal again because in his reproductive urge he destroys the possibility of attaining that measure of satisfaction and dignity necessary for his ennoblement? Will the twenty-first century witness a crescendo of violence as the direct product of congestion—a violence spreading indiscriminately over domestic and international life?

Such a Spenglerian view obviously encompasses more than the third world societies. Indeed, many of these societies are still relatively underpopulated, although extremes in the other direction like India are also to be seen. These are the societies, moreover, where controls or incentives for population control may be the most difficult to provide. I join those who believe that population control is as important an undertaking as any single action in the quest for peace in our time. It must be given the highest priority, for the quality of human life will bear an even closer correlation to those basic psychological and economic conditions that relate to the overarching questions of peace or war.

Whatever the trends with respect to population, however, the revolutions of production on the one hand and of expectations on the other will continue in their fascinating competition. Economic development, whether within a single state or among states, is certain to be uneven. Much has been written and spoken about the growing gap between the haves and have-nots, with the assumption always that the critical issues relate to the increasing separation between such societies as the United States and Indonesia, for example. It may well be, however, that in the coming decades uneven development within the third world will have the most significant political repercussions.

Already, the trend is well advanced. In some new nations, growth rates are extraordinarily high and the economic prospects are good. In other cases, the growth rates are satisfactory without being spectacular. But another group of new states is currently facing economic stagnation. Each of these situations poses its own specific political problems. We have discovered in the United States that after poverty ceases to be a class problem, pools of poverty (in our case, generally associated with ethnic minorities and depressed areas) continue to exist, helping to create political unrest. So it will presumably be in the third world. The problems of affluence now faced by us (and the Japanese, for example) are not necessarily less complex than those of poverty. States with very rapidly growing economies are likely to be the truly revolutionary societies, as we have emphasized, and their preoccupation with internal developments can have profound repercussions upon questions of global peace.

On the other hand, countries closely linked with the rest of the world via the variety of communications now existing may find that merely "satisfactory" economic growth rates are not sufficient to ward off political troubles (especially if an imbalance between the agrarian and industrial sectors prevails). An impatience, a demand for the end products of modernization immediately (and often, without a willingness to pay its costs) is likely to mount in such societies. This will be more likely if contacts with advanced societies are intimate.

Ironically, in the short run, the problems of stagnation may be the most manageable from a political point of view. A people struggling for survival, as has frequently been noted, rarely exhibit the greatest potential for revolution, and in any case, they rarely have the capacity by themselves to create a crisis far beyond their own borders. In the longer run, to be sure, stagnation or low economic growth is no prescription for political order or international peace. By the same token, however, it is vital to underline once again the fact that there is no clear correlation between economic development and domestic tranquility or a peaceful international order.

The crucial question of 1980 or 1990 may thus be, What is the relation between poverty-stricken Bagapola and neighboring Kanda, relatively dynamic and prosperous? As significant differences develop between neighboring states and regions, the gross picture of today will become at once more complex, and quite possibly more dangerous. This is not inevitable, to be sure. States with radically different levels of development and rates of growth have lived peacefully together as neighbors. But new types of problems frequently emerge when radical imbalances of growth commence. For example, witness the troubled relations between the United States and Mexico for nearly a century beginning in the 1840s.

At this point, it might be appropriate to draw certain conclusions from the themes advanced. First, there is no reason to believe that the era of small wars is coming to a close. On the contrary, such wars may well increase in number, and represent a growing problem to the world as a whole. Nationalism will continue to mount. Internal problems will remain grave and unsolved in many instances. The utility of having external opponents as scapegoats or distractions will continue to be substantial, both to satisfy ideological needs and those of practical politics. Small states, moreover, will acquire more sophisticated weapons, hence a greater capacity to defend themselves (or menace others); this very fact, however, will encourage all types of rebels within each state to look to external sources for material as well as moral support. In an age when the successful storming of the barricades is becoming ever more difficult, the premium of turning domestic conflict into international conflict naturally becomes higher, viewed from the standpoint of the dissident.

It is quite possible that the risk of nuclear confrontations between the major powers will continue to recede, at least the type of confrontation threatened in the early 1950s and again at the time of the Cuban missile crisis. Such a war promises no victors, no solutions, even temporary, to the gravest issues. Thus, the small war emanating from the problems of the third world is likely to constitute the most significant threat to peace in our time, especially when these problems are used by other states as a means of seeking to change the regional or global balance of power. It is also clear that although a major power like the United States has accepted the principle of limited war, this is not necessarily true of those states, whether of the second or third world, who do not bear equivalent responsibilities or hold equivalent power. For example, we are today confronting an opponent in North Vietnam who still preaches and practices total war, including a massive psychological-political campaign that carries into the heart of America. How does one juxtapose the requirements of limited war, when conflict is judged necessary, against the pursuit of total war by one's opponent?

Once again, we stand face to face with one of the great issues of today. In the absence of a viable international order, and in the face of those committed to a philosophy of international change through violence, peace has been heavily dependent in recent years upon two efforts: the establishment of political equilibrium in the most crucial regions of the world, namely Europe and East Asia, and the largely unilateral commitments of the most powerful nation in the world, the United States, whenever either of these equilibria was gravely threatened. Despite the criticisms directed against American policies over the past thirty years, historians of the future will record that it was American power—in all of its forms, economic, political, and military—that prevented massive wars in the extraordinarily troubled age that followed the end of Western domination of the world. And they will also record that it was fortunate in this age to have a nation which combined enormous power with a deep humanistic tradition, enabling it to give of itself abundantly while placing such limited demands upon the recipients. This is not to deny policy errors on the part of the U.S. government, or deficiencies in our political culture. But there is no reason, in my opinion, for the guilt complex that has become the stock-in-trade of some of our citizens.

Inevitably, however, the demands of the last three decades upon this nation, many coming from the third world, have produced problems for us and for others. Today, the clamor for a return to isolation in one form or another is growing. There is also a more ambiguous proposal that at first glance has very considerable merit, namely that our contribution to peaceful change can be encompassed in two forms: economic and technical assistance on the one hand, and the maintenance of a nuclear umbrella on the other. Both of these contributions are necessary, but I would suggest that they are not sufficient.

If small wars are indeed the most serious threat, neither technical aid nor the nuclear deterrent will meet the problem. At most, these commitments, particularly the latter, may help to contain the conflicts that ensue, but even this achievement is by no means certain. What is needed at present, as suggested earlier, is a means of defining and enforcing peaceful coexistence in a time when experimentation at all political levels is likely to be extensive, sometimes explosive. For our lifetime and beyond, we shall live with states having radically different sociopolitical institutions, different economic systems, and different ideological patterns. What constitutes interference on the part of one state in the internal affairs of another? What are the true differences between a conflict that is purely civil, and one that is international? What are the requirements if states having such basic differences are to live together without conflict? And most importantly, how and by whom are these requirements to be enforced?

The relationship between the third world and the prospects for peaceful change revolves in very considerable measure around the capacity of the first and second worlds to join in seeking answers to these questions, and in the establishment of multilateral mechanisms of inquiry, arbitration, and sanctions if necessary, when violations occur. It may be recalled that in the mid-1950s at the time of the Bandung Conference, a group of Asian nations, communist and noncommunist, did agree upon certain broad principles of peaceful coexistence. Subsequently, several of those very nations fell into strife with one another. The principles of Bandung were forsaken, and there was no international body adequate to probe the causes or suggest the remedies. If the third world is not to be a source of continuing threats to world peace, the basic political issues of our time must acquire as much importance as the economic and military ones. And fundamentally, the political issues of today that are crucial to international peace relate to the issue of peaceful coexistence in its fullest, most complex sense.

Clearly, there are no single solutions, no simple cure-alls to the issues of the late twentieth century. In one sense, for our own people the supreme challenge is to learn how to live with protracted insecurity at a time when we possess enormous power—hence, major responsibilities—and still preserve our democratic institutions. There is nothing necessarily eternal about democracy just as there is no convenient stopping point in that process which we call today modernization. How our future development will mesh with that of other societies, and how we can order priorities so that both domestic and international issues achieve their due share of attention and energy, are vital to many peoples, not just to Americans.

Thus far, these questions have been phrased rather crudely, as if the decision for us lay between being policeman to the world and total withdrawal. We have never been policeman to the world, nor should we be. And we could not withdraw totally from the world, even if we foolishly attempted to do so. The true challenge in considering both priorities and methods is to come abreast of the real issues of the present and future as they pertain to development, interstate relations, peace and war. It has been the thrust of this essay that trends in the third world require a combination of efforts in which we must play not a solo, but an important role: a renewed emphasis upon various types of suprastate organizations after basic changes have been considered and, in some cases, adopted; the acceptance of high levels of economic growth as essential; major attention to population controls; finally, a concentration upon the techniques of defining and enforcing peaceful coexistence.

As indicated at the outset, the world is not divided today into three component parts, and hence there is no third world in a precise sense. It is clear, however, that a major part of the globe today, whether measured in population or area, has only recently begun those political and economic tasks associated with modernization—a process which other societies commenced decades, even centuries ago. Some of these new states, moreover, are prepared to experiment with open political institutions—admittedly, a hazardous, difficult experiment—but also an important one, because pluralism makes the commitment to external violence on the part of any state more difficult.

Sometimes, it should be stated, third world spokesmen claim far more virtue, importance, or unity than is warranted. The major states, moreover, are now well aware of the frequent attempts at blackmail, or playing one force against another, that have been built into the policies of certain third world states. In many cases, tougher policies on the part of the major powers to counteract such tendencies are fully justified. It remains true, however, that the broad directions taken by the third world will influence the lives of us all, and relate directly to the overriding issue of peace in our time.

The Drive to Power

Bertrand de Jouvenel

We are convened to celebrate the fiftieth anniversary of a great institution; therefore, it seems proper to consider some striking phenomena of the past half-century.

THE MEANINGS OF POWER

As my assignment is "The Drive to Power," it would perhaps be useful to discuss first some of the meanings of "power." The word logically has an endless variety of meanings, since "power" and "possibility" have a common root and any possibility thus implies an adequate power. The most general meaning of the word is the capacity to produce effect. Thus we say that the power of an elephant is greater than that of a goat, or the power of a river greater than that of a neighboring stream. Power in that physical sense is certainly not foreign to our topic, as it is the main characteristic of our civilization to seek and use ever more power, and this is of major consequence in the political field.

Power as physical means to achieve concrete results is handled by men. The same power which was taken as a substantive in the preceding paragraph is now taken as an attribute of the handler. The power of an ox is now seen as the power of Peter, to whom the ox belongs, who uses the ox. In this sense, though Peter may be weaker than Paul, he has more power if he owns many oxen to Paul's one. There is therefore such a thing as proprietary power. However, this extends only over nonhuman means. Legally, Peter may use the forces of his oxen even as those of his own body, but in practice he cannot: if he has many pairs of oxen he will need the assistance of his sons or of servants to handle them.

And thus we come to the power made up of united human forces. The more forces combined, the greater the potential for achievement; but the actual efficiency of these collective forces depends upon their management. Merely additive efforts, such as those of oarsmen, are effective insofar as they are produced simultaneously in response to a signal. In the more interesting case of aggregative efforts, effectiveness depends upon the devising and observing of a distribution of tasks.

So in the case of human forces combined for achievement, the word "power" will occur in two different senses, referring on the one hand to the action the group as a whole is capable of exerting upon the outside world, and on the other hand to the action the leader and organizer of the group is capable of exerting upon it. The latter is managerial power, which in the past applied only in the private realm to domestic husbandry and in the public realm to the handling of armies.

Unquestionably, the major change in social structure over the last two centuries has been the increasing importance of organizations for economic purposes, each of which has involved more and more people and an ever more intricate architecture of tasks, therefore increasing the role of management. For most of this period, governments were achievement-oriented only in the realm of international power rivalry. The capacity to wage war successfully was important, implying the capacity to intimidate; this meant emphasis upon the potential of the army and navy which, in turn, meant managerial power over the paraphernalia of war and over manpower trained for war. But in the civil realm, governments were not achievement-oriented. It was not their business to lead and marshal the activities of subjects for positive results; it was their business only to regulate such activities, and this involved nothing more than law, justice, and police.

It is quite remarkable how insignificant police forces were in the late eighteenth century—and this independently of political regimes. We easily follow Thomas Paine's argument that the pressure of the citizenry itself is a suffcent means of enforcement if laws are made and decisions of justice rendered by ordinary citizens trusted and chosen by their fellows and responsive to public feeling. But it is striking to observe that also in monarchic France, where these conditions did not exist, Paris was policed on the eve of the Revolution by a civilian force of about two hundred, seconded by a military force of about one thousand.

It is disturbing to find that, again independently of political regimes, governments of our day seem to need enormously larger police forces. This is—in terms of resources—but a minute part of the "means to do" required by modern governments. The prodigious increase in their requirements is, of course, explained by their having assumed many important positive functions. The vogue of "planning-programming-budgeting" reflects the commitment of modern governments to a diversity of achievements. The pursuit of these achievements involves the input of resources to be handled for results; that is, the exercise of managerial power.

Thus, we find ourselves in an era of vast managerial power, some private and some public. In both cases there is need for its wise and prudent use. Also, a variety of pressures are brought to bear upon its use; and since there is a hunger for its capture, the temptation is great to press for power or to seize it by violent means. There is, indeed, some danger of the verification of Cournot's prediction uttered in 1861 that while administraton becomes more elaborate and scientific, politics becomes more crude. [1]

THE DRIVE TO POWER

Taking power first in the more general sense of the capacity to do, I find the title assigned to be admirably chosen to characterize the spirit of our specific civilization. I stress the adjective "specific" because however much of our culture may be rooted in the history of Europe previous to the nineteenth century, the civilization we live in today is almost as foreign to that which culminated in eighteenth century Europe as to Chinese or Indian civilization. It is a new civilization, reared on a new basis.

Every other civilization had accepted as its material basis the physical power immediately available—that of men, of animals and, to some degree, that of rivers or wind. That Western man did thirst for more power was manifested by his making better use than heretofore of wind and streams.

A new civilization was heralded with the publication in 1690 of Papin's memoir, *A New Method to Obtain Very Powerful Forces at a Low Price*. This title signifies the changing concept of using the forces immediately apparent to eliciting new forces; in other words, generating power. The very symbol of this power-seeking civilization is the nuclear plant where great power is spent to obtain far more power.

The material history of Western Europe and North America can properly be written in terms of the ever-increasing acquisition and spending of power. While power was limited, so was the realm of possibilities. Men had always thought in terms of limited possibilities, so it took quite a long time to dissolve that postulate and to bring about a general awareness that the frontier of possibilities was fast receding.

Images spark awareness. Thus the image of America served Europe and then the world. The vast and increasing possibilities were perceived in the simplest form: for example, the automobile at every door not only symbolized what may be called the individualized dividend of power but also represented the high average buying power of the individual. While the impact of this occurred long ago, recently the trip to the moon indicated the extent of the collective possibilities acquired.

Both something as trivial as the automobile and something as amazing as sending men to the moon rest upon the acquisition of power from nature. That is the quantitative requirement, the material cause. But if the automobile and its fuel are readily available, it is due to vast organizations of which such means of individualized power are outputs; and if men have walked on the moon, it is the outcome of an especially vast and intricate organization, the organization being the efficient cause. Thus, the history of our civilization appears as the joint product of a quantitative increase in physical power and a structural development of organizations.

Both these aspects of objective history could not fail to influence human attitudes. Take an artisan of the eighteenth century: moderation and self-reliance were traits which came naturally in view of his circumstances. Aware of the limits set by his means, he regarded achievement as dependent upon himself, so he could take pride in success or blame for failure. Not so our contemporary: to him possibilities are undefined, mediated by organizations upon which he feels dependent, and on which, therefore, center both his hopes and resentments.

OF ORGANIZATIONS

It is the essential structural characteristic of modern society that the means to do are concentrated in organizations. These are a pervading presence in our daily lives. Open your kitchen cupboard and the names of huge organizations spring at you. The powerful genii of our society nestle in this humble place, offering welcome services. The same names will be quoted to you for your investments. And it is so far assumed that you must belong to an organization that, in the United States, hotel forms ask you to list it, which reminds me of *nul homme sans seigneur*.

A social landscape of organizations is so familiar to us that there would be no point in mentioning it, were it not that our political ideas have been shaped mainly by seventeenth and eighteenth century authors to whom such a landscape was unknown and by whom it was unforeseen.

They thought of the means to do as dispersed among individuals, so much so that the independent mastery of the means, whether great or small, was to them a necessary condition of political rights. It followed that not only alms-takers and domestic servants but also wage-earners were excluded from political rights— and that even by the Levellers. Thus, their idea of the citizen was tied to a condition which has almost disappeared.

Organizations operating with concentrated means were not unknown to them. Indeed, one such organization played a major part in their lives: the church. But this concentration was to be done away with. The dissolution of church properties and the reversion to individual owners was a main tenet of all seventeenth and eighteenth century thinkers. Indeed what was done by Henry the Eighth of England was to be done far more completely by the French Revolution. And what the Revolution was to do brutally was but the outcome of a psychological attitude displayed in a royal ordinance dated as early as 1749, the preliminary statement of which was that assets should normally be in the hands of families.[2]

Our authors were not unaware that there had to be some organizations working with concentrated assets and extensive manpower, but they were extremely distrustful of such concentrations of power. A case in point is Adam Smith's treatment of the joint-stock company, which he regarded as suitable only to those trades of "which all the operations can be reduced to what is called a Routine, or to such a uniformity of method as admits of little or no variation."[3] This is so very different from what we know of corporations that Smith's statement calls for elucidation. This is offered by his follower McCulloch: "The business of a great association must be conducted by factors or agents; and unless it be of such a nature as to admit of their duties being clearly pointed out and defined, the association would cease to have any effectual control over them, and would be, in a great measure, at their mercy."[4] These statements clearly bring out the eighteenth century reluctance to *entrust the means of many to a few*, that is, to form a collected power; a reluctance resting on the fear that such collected power would lead to autonomy for the factors or agents.

It is apparent that if such fear prevailed in the case of private agents handling privately collected power, it was to be even stronger in the case of public agents handling publicly collected power. And indeed the whole idea of a "government of laws, not men" reflects the idea of public agents whose duties are so defined as to leave them almost no discretion. From which it followed that the government functions performed by the executive would be only routine operations.

This evokes the Athenian executive of the fifth century as depicted by Aristotle.[5] There was no unity of the executive but a variety of executive magistracies, each entrusted for a single year, each filled by the drawing of lots. This procedure of nomination meant that what the magistrate had to do was so programmed as to be feasible by anyone. A quite different system obtained for those entrusted with defense, whereby ten generals were elected and could be renewed in their functions: here it seemed necessary to look to qualities of leadership and to allow discretion.

What pertains to war has always been regarded as a special case, but limiting ourselves here to what does not, the theme that organizations can be run on routines should for a moment be studied. Quite puzzlingly we encounter this theme again as late as 1917 in Lenin's book *The State and Revolution*, in which he says the revolution will transform the whole of the productive apparatus into one great workshop and factory. The running of it, he says, calls for nothing more than "mere agents of execution of our directives, superintendents and accountants . . . functions of great simplicity which already are perfectly within the capacity of average town-dwellers, and which they can perform for workers' wages." There seems to be no inkling here of the problems of management. But before we go on to the managing of organizations and the theme of managerial power, let us consider for a moment the logic of eighteenth century distrust of concentrated power.

THE ANGLE OF DISCRETION

Compare a walker with the driver of a car. The latter can cover a far greater distance in a day. Take their respective ranges as radii of two circles, and these two circles as representative of their respective powers. Now consider that the walker cannot by mere walking be a danger to anyone; not so the driver. Therefore, the use which the driver makes of a far greater power must be regulated. He may not use his car at certain speeds or in certain ways. Let us represent these restrictions upon his physical power by shaded areas of the circle. The walker's circle is small but wholly unshaded; the driver's circle is large but only partly unshaded. The relation of the permissible to the possible has declined. This can be expressed in terms of an angle which I call "the angle of discretion." It seems to me it has been a maxim of all times that the greater the power, the greater should be the restrictions upon its use. In other words, the smaller the angle of discretion.

It is, however, the fate of all general principles that, according to circumstances, they are convenient to this or that interest. In the Middle Ages it was very convenient to the church and the lords that the monarch was so short of means that it was almost superfluous to keep down his angle of discretion, which the electors of the Germanic Emperor compressed to an extreme.

Absolute monarchy entailed a great rise both in the means of the monarch and in his angle of discretion, and this power led to a social transformation. But a new demand then arose for the narrowing of the angle of discretion, and whatever the inspiration thereof it cannot be doubted that such a narrowing in fact served the interests of men of property. The interplay of interests and principles is not my subject here. Whatever the causes, the history of government power from the time of the American Constitution to the war of 1914 was marked by two traits:

1. There was reluctance to entrust vast means to the executive.

2. Circumstances made it necessary to entrust ever-increasing means, but as Tocqueville noted and foresaw, there was a sharp concern to close the angle of discretion for the use of these means.

Thus, public agents entrusted with public power were under quite a different regime from private agents entrusted with private power. To these latter let us now pay some attention.

MANAGERIAL POWER

If means when concentrated were used in no other manner than when dispersed, their concentration would be favorable only to the concentrator, generating no material increase for society as a whole. Therefore, when the wise men of Israel denounced the man "who adds field to field" we can back such moral indignation with mundane common sense. This concentration added nothing to the overall social product while it hindered its distribution, and it impaired political union by discontenting many for the contentment of one. The concentration of means, therefore, can be justified in terms of the social interest only if it results in a productivity gain, whatever the kind of output to which it applies.

But whatever the social gain obtained by an act of concentration, there will be no futher gain if the agents to whom the concentrated means are entrusted are bound to a routine by the close prescriptions of their constituency. If they are reduced to the function of overseers, they can obtain from the concentrated means no more than an unchanging output, or an output fluctuating without trend as hard-driving and easy-going taskmasters alternate. This is an extremely undesirable state of affairs in moral and social terms since it puts a premium on hard-driving taskmasters; it need not be stressed what sufferings were inflicted in the early industrial age because it was seen that pressure brought to bear upon men (and indeed children, as denounced by Owen) produced results.

This detestable way of getting more output from "a power of men," to repeat the archaic but telling expression, can be eliminated by planning their activities; this was well known in terms of using soldiers for victory long before the problem arose of using workers in combination with fueled machines. So that, whether we refer to Athens or the Roman Republic or the Italian republics, far more discretion was granted to generals than to civil magistrates.

Similarly, when concentrated means were entrusted to an agent for productive purposes by a private constituency of shareholders, it was recognized that in order for progress to be made he had to be granted the discretion denied in the Smithian formula. Rather than a deliberate recognition, however, this was an unconscious imitation of the condition of the individual owner-manager.

No matter how undeliberate the move, it was momentous. A society which had enormously stressed individual property rights was thereby committed to recognize the owner's right to the free use of his own means. The transfer of most of this discretion to an agent generated massive powers in society.

That the political authorities allowed these huge powers to develop over the protests of the wielders of individual means reveals that the psychological climate surrounding the political constituency was changing, that the constituency was increasingly taking on the character of a collection of consumers interested in obtaining more goods and, therefore, favorable to the structures which proved more productive. While men as buyers were favorable, men as wage-earners had no more reason to be resentful of the corporation than of the individual owner. And Marxian socialism told them that the greater the concentration of means, the fewer the masters, and the easier the taking over of the means of production by the constituency of workers would be.

The historic elements of the acceptance of power concentration in the economic realm can best be observed, dramatically compressed in a few years, on the French scene. Up to World War II France had retained a very high proportion of individual wielders of individual resources: peasants, artisans, small traders, small industrialists. These people who alone would have qualified as citizens in the eyes of seventeenth and eighteenth century authors are today universally condemned as holding back the overall progress of national output.

Now let me note the political consequences of this great change in economic structure.

POLITICAL POWER CATCHES UP

This structural phenomenon had gone a long way in the most industrialized countries—Britain, Germany, and the United States—in the latter half of the nineteenth century. At the same time, eighteenth century doctrines still prevailed in the political field. It was still felt that public authorities should be entrusted with the least possible means and that their use should be tied down as closely as possible.

Concerning the mere volume of means, the following figures seem telling: in 1890 public expenditures in Britain (central and local), exclusive of war-related expenditures, were less than 5 per cent of GNP.[6] Public employment (central and local) was less than 2 per cent of total working population.[7] But even more important was the tying down of the means. To put it bluntly, government was an eighteenth century edifice, suitable to rule an eighteenth century social landscape but dwarfed by the social landscape at the end of the nineteenth century.

Such weakness of public authority relative to social power had also been a feature of the late Middle Ages, mainly in relation to the church but also with regard to temporal power. From that previous disproportion arose what we call absolute monarchy. While historical analogies should never be pressed too far, it is worth stressing that the rise of absolute monarchy took not only the quantitative form of an increase in public means but the qualitative form of a great increase in public discretion. It does seem to me that the same two phenomena are the principal political characteristics of the twentieth century.

I wish to concentrate on the qualitative change. This I have elsewhere ventured to call a shift, more or less pronounced, from a nomocratic character of government to a telocratic character. I call Nomocracy a regime wherein government is mainly conceived as seeing to the observance by citizens of general rules, and Telocracy a regime wherein government is mainly conceived as striving to achieve future goals. It seems to me that the term "executive power," which I believe to have been coined by Locke, corresponds to a function of execution in a nomocratic regime and, indeed, some evidence for this connotation of subordination is offered by the fact that in the British Civil Service the executive class ranks second to the administrative class. It seems to me, therefore, that in our day one should not speak of "the executive power" but of "the active power."

Now this active public power bears a strong resemblance to private managerial power. Even as managerial power justifies itself by results, so does governmental power. And the entrusting of a powerhouse to a manager or managerial team is based in each case upon the belief in their capacity to achieve.

THE ERA OF MANAGERIAL GOVERNMENTS

That we are in an era of managerial governments cannot be doubted, nor are these governments limited to socialist countries. For instance, President Nixon's Executive Order of July 1969 clearly implies that government is to systematically pursue national goals by managerial methods. This is not a surprising development. When society was static it was the government's obvious duty to maintain a known order. In a progressive society, the government is called upon to ensure an expected rate of economic progress, to remedy social evils which arise from change, and to provide the social benefits which do not flow from market mechanisms. This is the more complex part of government management; it is far more difficult to handle urban problems than to ensure a certain regularity of economic growth.

Governments increasingly assume tasks which are not regulatory but pragmatic. However, they are hampered therein by a long-standing tradition that all manner of public servants must be closely bound by detailed instructions. And the tradition is such that even if the head of a department or agency is granted a considerable degree of discretion, it seldom travels down the line. Actual field operators must follow the instructions given; they enjoy no flexibility and they may not report their experiences, or disappointments met with, or discontents aroused.

Public agencies, at least in Europe, seem bereft of any feedback mechanism procuring adjustment to the reactions of the public. It follows that such reactions build up into recriminations which have to be carried up to the headquarters of the department or agency, if not to a higher level. The greater the undertakings of government the more its operating structures stretch throughout the body politic, and the greater the volume and variety of complaints assailing it. That is, of course, in the case of a regime which shows proper respect for freedom of expression—where elected representatives lend their voices, and communications media their channels, to all manner of complaints, and where, moreover, people can demonstrate their displeasure. Under such conditions the handling of vast powers is not dangerous to freedom, nor is it enviable. What is dangerous, however, is the thought that comes into some minds, such as came into that of young Bonaparte on August 10, 1792: "I would not let them do this to me." The galleon of state, that vast treasureship of means, may be enviable to such a mind if it can be seized by a crew willing to use it regardless of reactions. We cannot but observe the increasing frequency of such events; their starting point is to be found in World War I.

TOTALITARIANISM OUT OF TOTAL WAR?

The rise of totalitarian governments has been a major feature of European history in the past half-century. This phenomenon was totally unexpected by those who at the end of the nineteenth century formulated pictures of the century to come. They looked for a liberalization of political institutions in those countries that had not yet made parliament supreme and individual liberties safe from arbitrary measures.

The blame for the occurrence of totalitarian regimes has been laid by the famous historian Elie Halévy at the door of the statesmen ruling civilized Europe in 1914. As I mentioned before, in those days the executive was generally held on a short leash. Only in foreign affairs did he enjoy great discretion, and this latitude was used disastrously. The statesmen of Europe stumbled into the Great War, the most purposeless, meaningless war in history, a major calamity for which, in my opinion, all players were jointly responsible. Not only did they stumble into it but they proved so inept as to be incapable of climbing out of this morass of blood spilled in vain.

From this misuse of discretion arose discretionary powers unheard of, even undreamed of. In the eighteenth century the concern of European society had been to make "peace more of peace and war less of war," as Burke admirably put it. [8] Here war was made more of war. The Romans of the Republic had known enough to keep civil institutions and practices *intra muros* unchanged in time of war. Indeed, only after the Consul had marched out of the city limits could he don the red vestment of war and wield its discipline. In World War I, on the contrary, our leaders did their utmost to inject the discipline of war into civil society. Indeed those who were unfit to fight or to forge arms were induced to make up these deficiencies with expressions of hatred.

It has been strikingly stated by Elie Halévy:

> The era of tyrannies dates from August 1914, in other words from the moment when the belligerent nations adopted a regime which can be defined as follows:
>
> a)   in the economic realm, state control far extended all means of production and distribution, with appeals from governments to union leaders for help in this program—thus unionism and corporatism as well as statism;
>
> b)   in the intellectual realm, state control of thought, taking two forms: the one negative by the suppression of all expressions of opinion deemed against the national interest; the other positive, by what I shall term the "organization of enthusiasm." [9]

It is Halévy's point that the will to wage total war brought about this dual conscription of means and minds, which set up the model of totalitarian regimes.

It is an irony of history that these models were set up in France and Britain, nations and governments held as paragons of liberalism, no less than in Germany, which, for all the fancies and posturings of the Kaiser, was a country of liberal practices.

That such a degree of control could be established over human actions and expressions, and with such ease, in the very countries which had been the historic leaders in establishing and securing liberties, offered striking proof of the weakness of the spirit of liberty, and of the potential tolerance of such control. And (this is the core of Halévy's thesis), it offered a strong temptation to any who, for various purposes, might want to establish such a system as permanent. According to Halévy's view, all the diverse totalitarian regimes which arose in Europe after 1914, and up to his exposition of 1936, stemmed from the "demonstration effect" of the war regime.

SOCIALIZATION OF MEANS
DISTINGUISHED FROM CONTROL OF MIND

In his important thesis, Halévy seems to put the direction imparted to economic resources and the direction imparted to individual attitudes on the same footing. I cannot agree with this.

The assumption by government of the means of production that had previously been concentrated by a capitalist process was an old socialist demand. In 1848 it figured in the Programme de Luxembourg, drafted by Louis Blanc and his associates,[10] with the interesting proviso that where firms were small (the case in all but a very few forms of activity) the individual owner would be bought off by the state, and ownership turned over to the collectivity of workers; both state capitalism and the cooperative anarcho-syndicalist solution were contained here, and it was clearly seen that some powers of coordination would have to be exercised. While Marx always refused to spell out socialist organization, his basic maxim that socialism would rise of itself out of capitalist evolution does indicate that he saw socialism as the supreme outcome of the process of concentration of means.

The Fabian Society, which was formed in the year following the death of Marx, received from the hands of Bernard Shaw its formulator of doctrine, Sydney Webb, of whom Shaw says: "As an upper civil servant, he saw that in state enterprise and ownership there was an alternative of capitalism."[11] Indeed, the idea of state ownership of control was ancient, well established, and thriving before 1914. It stood in a great many minds as a credible historical development, whether strongly desired or unwelcome.

This was not the case with the control of minds, nor the imposition of an orthodoxy, with its attendant inquisitions and police punishments. No one before 1914 desired or feared this. It did not figure as a credible historical development. It was not feared even by those who were antagonistic to the possible triumph of socialism. However dark the picture they drew, the policeman did not loom therein as a major character.

In the thoughtful essays of Emile Faguet,[12] we can find what a keen and impartial observer, in personal touch with socialist leaders of his day, saw as the probable socialist regime. The easygoing tempo then characteristic of public organizations would spread to all. Whatever the nominal authority of government over the whole, and within any part of an establishment, the balance of power would shift away from the head to the members. The members would not be dismissable, could not be driven, and could not be offered inducements that might generate an unwelcome inequality. The natural conservatism of the bulk of members would set an obstacle to innovations and reorganizations which could not then be justified by the requirements of competition. Socialism would be inconvenient, leading to a flabby economy. Such was the unfrightening nature of the danger.

Such a preview of socialism does not seem to me to have been unwarranted. I have suggested in my *Art of Conjecture* an Uchronian picture of a collective economy which would have been instituted in the earliest years of our century first in Britain and/or the United States, countries which had strong traditions of individual liberty and local self-government, which were the most advanced countries (as Marx had expected) and therefore had no urge to "catch up"; countries which furthermore were so placed geographically as to be relatively unworried by external menaces. Whether it would have worked out well is one question, and a quite different one from its bringing in its train a high degree of political constraint and punishment.

PARTITION OF THE WORLD
IN TERMS OF ECONOMIC OR POLITICAL INSTITUTIONS

This brings me to discuss the visions of world partition which arose when the United States and the Soviet Union fell out at the end of World War II.

It is socialist doctrine that all social institutions and practices are "superstructures" dependent upon economic practices and institutions. Therefore, the Russians are consistent in defining a socialist camp as one made up of those countries where there is public ownership of productive assets.

On the other hand it is liberal doctrine that the essential institutions and practices are those which guarantee the liberties of the subject and allow him full play as a citizen to freely express his opinions, to criticize his government and seek to influence it or, by legal means, to replace it. The American establishment would therefore have been consistent in defining the "free world" as made up of those countries where such liberties were secure and such rights were exercised.

A monumental error of judgment was made—if I may say so—by the American establishment when it accepted the Sovet view of world partition and applied the term "free world" indiscriminately to all countries where a socialist regime did not exist, however bad the actual condition of freedom in some of them; for instance in Greece of the colonels and Iraq of the hangings!

In so doing the American establishment offered a most effective weapon of anti-American propaganda. This can be formulated as follows: Judge them by their own choices. They are quite willing to forget about political liberty, provided the freedom of capitalist enterprise exists: this, then, is what they really stand for.

Now, whatever the effective merits of the contrasting economic systems, it is a fact that the general idea of socialism is more immediately appealing in most parts of the world than the general ideas of capitalism. So the American establishment accepted the placing of the contrast on a ground unfavorable to itself. But while this was a bad strategical move, a minor point to me, it was also a fundamental mistake. The contrast which really matters does not lie in economic institutions. Who would say, "Give me private corporations or give me death!"? The true contrast lies in political rights.

There were in Russia a few courageous men and women who publicly protested against the invasion of Czechoslovakia. See how they were treated. It is natural that they were few, as they knew what harsh punishment awaited them. Compare the treatment of American protestors against the Vietnam war at its worst, in the police handling of demonstrators at the Chicago Convention. This deplorable incident offers two proofs of political liberty: first that the demonstrators were allowed to assemble, while a painstaking political police would have nipped their plan in the bud; second that their harsh treatment aroused a storm of protest throughout the nation.

What was it that brought such a climate of joy to Czechoslovakia in the spring of 1968? Was it the prospect of reverting to capitalist institutions? It was the disappearance of censorship, the liquidation of the political police. And what was it that alarmed the powers of the Warsaw Pact? Indeed, the very same thing which had alarmed the powers of the Holy Alliance assembled at Troppau in November 1820 to take stock of the liberal revolutions which had taken place in Spain, Portugal, and Naples. They declared themselves "entitled to take foresightful measures to quell the spirit of unrest, the more so in view of the chances of its propagation." For this reason they called to account the King of Naples who had bowed to a bloodless rising and transmitted his powers to his son; after this meeting at Laibach, an Austrian army entered the Kingdom of Naples in March 1821.

There is not the slightest similarity between the social regimes of 1820 in the countries which participated in the Holy Alliance and those of 1968 in the countries which participated in the Warsaw Pact. And yet there is a striking similarity in their political behavior. This by itself refutes the Marxian tenet that political regimes are a mere reflection of economic institutions.

Incidentally, it also refutes those anti-Socialists who are unconscious Marxists. They regard an oppressive political regime as naturally resulting from public ownership of productive assets; and in so doing they merely transpose the statement of Marx (in his *Civil War in France*) that an oppressive political regime is of necessity bound to concentrated private ownership of assets. And the two opinions are equally based upon circumstantial evidence. It is a matter of historical record that in the days of Marx the law was all in favor of the employer and left him free to deal with his workers from economic strength, and that the police were at the beck and call, so to speak, of the employer. This was momentous but also momentary. It is not so in the capitalist countries of our day which have democratic political institutions. From this change we learn that coercive institutions and practices are not of necessity bound to public ownership. It will be clear that my purpose here is not to plead for socialism; rather it is to plead for turning our attention to the theme of political liberty or constraint in its own right.

It is in order here to stress that, if police means were strongly used in a large part of the nineteenth century in favor of rising capitalism, they had been used far more forcibly in earlier days in the service of another institution, the church. So the maintenance of orthodoxy, a motivation quite foreign to the economic realm, appears in history as a main motive for tyranny. And the role it plays in the character of government in the communist countries is obvious enough. That men in the twentieth century should propose to establish and maintain an orthodoxy would have seemed quite incredible to Europeans of 1913.

POLITICAL SURPRISES

It has been pointed out by Peter Drucker that an economist put to sleep in 1913 and awakened in our day would not be greatly surprised by the overall economic growth which has occurred, and, one may add, by the development of social institutions which has taken place in the advanced capitalist countries in legislation, social security, and union power.

A political scientist, however, would be surprised. What would surprise him least is the rise in governmental power. Such a quantitative increase had been proceeding in the quarter century up to World War I. It has certainly gone much farther than our political scientist would have predicted, but two great wars and the Great Depression have helped it along. On this score his surprise would attach only to the degree.

He would be more surprised by what I have called a qualitative change, that is, the great accentuation of the managerial character of government, attended by a reversal of the relative importance of the executive and parliament. Indeed, as late as 1929, a noted constitutionalist [13] stressed that the constitutions written since the war consecrated the loss of independence of the executive:

"Everywhere," said he, "it is parliament which forms the government." This feature, he explained, was a well-established custom in the classical abodes of parliamentarian institutions. But some new constitutions formalized this relationship, and, he noted, "it is in virtue of articles of the constitution that parliament nominates the ministers (Austria) or only the Prime Minister (Prussia)." The latter example brings to mind the election of Goering to that office.

Whatever the constitutions said, the aftermath of World War I was not an accentuated dependency of the executive upon parliament but quite the reverse. Even if he left out of account what occurred during the interwar period, our political scientist would regard the present state of affairs, even in countries such as Britain and France, as unexpected in view of 1913 trends. He would probably not regard it as illogical in view of the accentuation of the managerial functions of government, but he might well wonder at the absence of new constitutional doctrines pertaining to these new circumstances. However, his surprise on the score of the quantitative increase of means and his even greater surprise on the score of the qualitative change of functions would be dwarfed by his amazement at the change of attitude to public authority.

THE CHANGE OF ATTITUDE TO PUBLIC AUTHORITY

Public authority has enormously gained in fascination and lost in respectablility. It has gained in fascination because it has become so loaded with power. This formidable increase has very different justifications for economically advanced and economically retarded countries. In the case of the former, the progress due to the operations of larger and more efficient private organizations has called for an equilibrating progress in realms not well served by their activities.* In the case of countries where economic progress has not been achieved for lack of indigenous private organizations, the task of economic growth has been assigned to the authorities. And the very use of the term "social mobilization" to designate their mission is suggestive of military powers.†

*As the energy of private organizations is unquestionably what has made the difference between economic progress and economic backwardness, it would be of interest to inquire whether their activities could have created fewer social problems and left fewer needs unattended to. As these are in essence chartered bodies, would a difference of legal concepts have made an important practical difference?

†Thus Karl Deutsch comments, "Social mobilization can be defined as the process in which major clusters of old social, economic, and psychological commitments are eroded or broken and people become available for new patterns of socialization and behavior. As Edward Shils has rightly pointed out, the original images of 'mobilization' and of Mannheim's 'fundamental democratization' imply two distinct stages of the process: 1. the stage of uprooting or breaking away from old settings, habits, and commitments; and 2. the induction of the mobilized persons into some relatively stable new patterns of group membership, and commitment. In this fashion soldiers are mobilized *from* their homes and families and mobilized *into* the army in which they then serve." Karl Deutsch, "Social Mobilization and Economic Development," *American Political Science Review* (September 1961).

The fascination exercised by this great concentration of power takes different forms in different countries. In rich countries with liberal institutions and freedom to demand, the concentration of power leads to a concentration of expectations. Every man expects the powers that be to do their duty, that is, increase his possibilities. The powers are horns of plenty and it is important to each group to jockey for position; but the horns are also to be shaken if too little is obtained from them. Expectations and resentments center on established authorities, which are deemed increasers and distributors of possibilities. The attitude of the customer predominates over that of the citizen.

The responsible citizen, as he figures in political theory, is assumed to judge the actions of government by comparison with what he would do if he had to make the choices for all. This, however, requires a degree of information and attention which becomes unobtainable as the business of government becomes more complex.

The thoughtful attitude of the citizen depends upon the opportunity and habit of participating in the settlement of problems of which he has personal knowledge. And this, of course, wanes as decision-making recedes from local agencies to distant central organizations. While this is said to increase the efficiency of government, it diminishes the sympathy toward its wielders.

As practical involvement in public decision-making declines, moral involvement develops. Let me use for illustration three successive generations. The grandfather regrets the passing of the day when he could share in the control of public affairs, locally run; the father is adjusted to pressure politics; the grandson, struck by the immensity of powers, is scandalized by what seems to him to have been done wrongfully and by what has been left undone. For different reasons and to different degrees, the three generations tend to lose their respect for government.

Now turning to the countries where liberal institutions do not exist or are not well established, the fascination of power works in a different way: there the temptation to seize this great treasureship of means prevails. Returning to our political scientist awakened from his 1913 sleep, he would be impressed by the U.N. General Assembly, but then he would be shocked to learn how many of the high-minded speakers represent governments which were installed by violence. The most scandalous scene I have witnessed was that on television, of the Western ambassadors rushing to pay their compliments to a newly installed ruler and, in their haste, stepping over the unremoved corpses of the predecessor's bodyguard.

Guglielmo Ferrero, writing in 1942, stressed that as the principle of dynastic legitimacy was the basis on which Europe had been reestablished after the Napoleonic turmoil, so the principle of elective legitimacy was the principle on which world order would be reestablished after the Hitlerian turmoil. How much of this legitimacy—or of any other—is there in our world today?

Another feature which would strike our awakened political scientist is that the stablest governments of our day are, alas, those which have proved most vigilant in repressing freedom of expression. The statesman with the longest record of individual power in the world today is General Franco; the team with the longest record is, of course, that which rules Russia.

CONCLUSION

We are privileged to live in countries where political power is neither obtained by violent capture nor maintained by the stifling of opposition. It seems to me strange that we should be unworried that such countries are so few in our day. The liberals of the 1820s looked with complete confidence to the spreading of free institutions, and their confidence was, in fact, justified; things moved that way up to 1914. Do we feel any similar confidence today? Apparently we do not. If the Prague revolt aroused our hopes, its crushing was accepted with surprising equanimity.

Does anyone remember the proclamation of human rights at the inception of the United Nations? Certainly, it has no relevance to the standing of the several countries in the United Nations, nor does it affect the diplomatic relations of the countries where such rights are, in fact, observed. We take the world as it is or as it becomes, and deal with it in terms of expediency. But do we not, thereby, devalue the principles which are our own?

If we have no expectation of things changing our way, does it not imply the possibility of our changing the other way? That liberal regimes are in so small a minority in the present world should remind us that such regimes are not pre-ordained in the course of history but rather are a precious contrivance. What history does attest is that they may well disappear, as in the case of the Italian republics. We should be far more concerned than we are with this possibility; and we should pay far more attention to warding it off.

—4—

Man's Natural Desire for Peace

F. Hilary Conroy

Discussing man's natural desire for peace places me immediately in the role of Pollyanna of the conference. We have already been introduced to the reality of the drive for power, and in subsequent sessions we shall be meeting other realities equally unpleasant: wars, revolutions, rebellions, economic deprivation. Indeed, if we had the stomach for it we could easily spend the entire conference listing cruel examples of man's inhumanity, all firmly recorded in history. Not only that, but it can easily be shown that these are by no means limited to the distant past. They have reached new heights, or rather depths, of viciousness in the twentieth century, thus eliminating any idea of progress unless it be downward.

Previous Pollyannas, at least in the historical profession, have been consigned to oblivion. The last serious one, perhaps, was Edward P. Cheyney of my own University of Pennsylvania, who in his presidential address to the American Historical Association (1923) proclaimed six laws of history impelling mankind toward democracy, peace, and moral progress.[1] War he explained away by saying its causes were becoming increasingly just, like making the world safe for democracy. It might serve as an in-joke among historians to say the idea that the course of history reveals progress toward a peaceful and enlightened human society was buried with J. B. Bury, who published a book on the subject in 1932.[2] Perhaps it could be said that only fools and physicists believe in progress today. However, we are discussing here only man's desire for peace, not attempting to prove that he has made any progress toward it.

In the process of studying East Asian history, which became my main field of scholarly inquiry, I studied quite a bit of Confucianism, Taoism, Buddhism, and Shintoism in their assorted forms, but more in terms of the history of their development and influence on the social and political systems of the countries of Eastern Asia than for the intrinsic merit of their ideas. Recently, however, I have been reviewing my Oriental philosophy, looking for some eternal truths contained therein. One of these, it now appears, may be man's natural desire for peace, and perhaps even better, a latent potential for attaining it. I shall try first to make a case for this from philosophy, then, if possible, buttress it from history.

For our excursion into philosophy, let us begin with a quotation from the *New York Times* of March 12, 1969, of a prayer issued by the Dalai Lama on the tenth anniversary of his flight from Tibet to escape Chinese Communist rule. He said, "Our compassion goes to those who destroy both themselves and others. Help those rough and cruel ones gain the eye of wisdom . . . help them gain loving kindness and a pitying mind." On the future of Buddhism among Tibetan refugees, now widely scattered in exile, he added that if Tibetans realize that Buddhism is sanctioned by reason and logic, they will retain their faith, but if they rely only on the sanctions of tradition, the materialism of the modern world will draw them away. [3]

How can the Dalai Lama presume to talk about an "eye of wisdom" and the "sanction of reason and logic" for something as esoteric and mysterious as Tibetan Buddhism? In 1966 a new book on Tibetan Buddhism appeared, entitled *Tibetan Buddhism Without Mystification*,[4] by Herbert V. Guenther, a scholar trained at the Universities of Munich and Vienna, who has lived and studied with Tibetan monks and scholars, and has had access to textual materials hitherto unknown in the West. From his book, we can for the first time gain some appreciation of what the best minds of Tibet have been trying to say over the centuries, and it is of great importance to our present subject.

The main points are these. Though it has become customary to see man as a chain in the link of living things, one among many (here we might put our Western concept of evolution alongside the Eastern one of reincarnation), he is nevertheless *unique* in certain kinds of (higher) mental processes,[5] at least as things stand here and now and have stood since the dawn of history. Ortega y Gasset was getting at the same idea when he wrote:

> If we do not know what man is going to be, we can discover what he is not going to be. Man lives in view of the past. . . . The tiger of today is neither more nor less a tiger than was that of a thousand years ago; it is being a tiger for the first time; it is always a first tiger. But the human individual is not putting on humanity for the first time. . . . Man is not a first man, an eternal Adam; he is formally a second man, a third man, etc. [6]

Man can learn, but, says Tibetan Buddhism, learning is a process which is by no means automatic. Most people by the time they reach adulthood are thoroughly stained (have acquired bad karma), either from past lives or from present surroundings. Victimized by emotionality, wishfulness, and a peculiar sort of intellectual fog, they are in fact only men in their inferior nature, with a long way to go before achieving full humanity. To be conquered are the hellish emotions, hatred, cravings, greed, ferocity, and jealousy; wishfulness, which includes all forms of utopianism; and the intellectual fog, which proves to be the subject-object mode of thinking. [7] This prevents them from apprehending things and persons as they are because they think of them only as they contribute to a purpose. (We note in passing the similarity to Buber's I-Thou versus I-It relationship, Kant's observation that we see things as our mind defines them in categories, and Marx's that we see things not only in categories but according to use, thus moving even further away from objectivity. [8])

However, there is a way (a path) to correct these inadequacies and to move from inferior to mediocre and thence on to the level of a superior man, untroubled by them and able then to accomplish much. The principles by which this may be accomplished are not so mysterious. Emotionality (or emotivity) is to be eliminated, not by repressing the emotions but by counteracting each with its opposite, thus hate with love, ferocity with passivity; wishfulness or utopianism and the egoistic subject-object view of things may be countered with attention to "unknowing" and to relativity. [9] Certainly those concepts should not be beyond the average educated person of the present time, though putting them into practice may be another matter. They add up to a kind of gentle world perspective, the acquisition of which makes one a mediocre man. Perhaps most of us are mediocre already—that is unless our IQ's are too high, in which case we have something special to overcome; Guenther points out that although intelligence is required, it is not the sort which can be measured quantitatively and scores well on tests. [10]

Having become mediocre, a man should next develop a solid foundation in four topics: the uniqueness of human existence; its transitoriness through death; the relation between the cause and effect of one's actions; and the general unsatisfactoriness of the world. Lest this seem too easy, let us ponder how much or how little of our educational experience was really concerned with these matters. Certainly they should be covered in a liberal arts education, but are they? The death theme seems especially neglected in America. I recall one Orientalist saying that we might get in proper perspective by referring to ourselves from college age onward as the dying instead of the living. It jolts one.

At any rate the least one can learn from a study of these subjects is that since life is short, and suffering is in abundance, one should not add to the suffering. [11] Having learned this one becomes a superior man. One has acquired the "Real View." One may do more, much more, especially if one becomes truly enlightened, but that is not necessary for the proposition at hand, man's natural desire for peace. The desire for peace (leaving aside the modifier "natural" for a moment) is certain to be a key, if not the key principle, with the superior man, according to Tibetan Buddhism. It is likely also that it will be a very important principle with the mediocre man, given the world-perspective he is expected to attain.

As for the word "natural," I feel that this cannot be sustained in the sense of born into, but the desire for peace becomes natural (necessary, certain) as soon

as a (not too difficult to reach) way of knowing is attained. This is spoken of in Buddhist terms as the "path of seeing," by which is meant simply perceiving things and people in a manner free of emotive categorization, and as the "path of attending to be seen,"[12] by which the subject-object dichotomy is abolished. More simply, we see ourselves as others (should) see us, assuming they utilize "the path of seeing." Hence, all that is needed is an undistorted view of others and ourselves, and the desire for peace emerges. What could be more "natural" than that?

From the previous discourse we should now understand why the Dalai Lama need ask only that "the rough and cruel ones" obtain "the eye of wisdom." If they could only see clearly, their compassion would arise out of wisdom and their reliance on violence would cease. Of course, how to get the waves of compassion going and to get those rough and cruel ones, the inferior men—in which category all power seekers and hence most of the world's leaders[13] would fall—to reach even the take-off stage of mediocrity is the sixty-four-dollar question. Tibetan Buddhism has answers for this, but before we consider them let us glance briefly at some other philosophic traditions.

It may here be asked why we use Tibetan Buddhism as our philosophic anchor point. The answer is that it has been a sophisticated, yet relatively isolated phenomenon. It is sophisticated in that it has distilled, or thought about intensively and objectively, teachings originally derived from India; and it is isolated in being completely separated from the Western philosophic tradition and also from the Chinese, at least in the early centuries. We turn now to those independent variables for possible verification of what Tibetan Buddhism has taught us.

Independently of Buddhist and Western thought, Chinese thinkers produced some fascinating ideas but unfortunately to date there has appeared no Guenther to present them "without mystification." James Legge produced the classic and still standard translation of the Confucian canon during the decade 1861-1872, and though there have been many revisions, elaborations, and interpretations, they still have the flavor of the peculiar and the anecdotal about them. However, in the Doctrine of the Mean (Chung Yung) particularly, but also in the Analects (Lun Yü) and the so-called Great Learning (Ta Hsüeh) are certain points pertinent to our theme, which tend to reinforce the Tibetan position that through learning (correctly "without error") man comes naturally to desire peace.

The Doctrine of the Mean deals with the mind, and at the same time with the "universe." The main idea is that the mind in its fully developed form is a kind of mirror or negative (in the photographic sense) of the universe, and hence in its decisions the cultivated (superior) mind will take into account a universal perspective. What results then is "harmony." In Legge's translation, "When there are no stirrings of pleasure, anger, sorrow, or joy the mind may be said to be in the state of Equilibrium. When those feelings have been stirred and they act in

their due degree, there ensues what may be called the state of Harmony. This equilibrium is the great root from which grow all the human actings in the world, and thus Harmony is the universal path which they all should pursue. Let the states of equilibrium and harmony exist in perfection, and a happy order will prevail through heaven and earth, and all things will be nourished and flourish."[14] Thus the cultivated mind is the "rolled up" universe. The superior man does not join; he encircles.[15]

Chapter XIII of the Doctrine of the Mean emphasizes that this path is "not far" from man. "When men try to pursue a course, which is far from the common indications of consciousness, this course cannot be considered the [correct] path."[16] This is because the "cultivated principle of human nature" is Shu (forgiveness, indulgence, mercy). Legge goes on to sum up this section with the famous "What you do not like when done to yourself, do not do to others."[17]

The last part of the Doctrine of the Mean, from chapter 20, part 18, is largely a discourse on Ch'eng (sincerity, guilelessness, truth). The written character is made up of two parts, words and completion. The argument is that words (and concepts) must be restored to their true meanings. Words in ordinary use are invented for a purpose, not to describe things as they are in themselves. (Calling a killing an execution and a War Department a Defense Department are certainly examples of this.) But the cultivated mind can "rectify" names, and more than that, with "sincerity" a union is effected between the external and the internal[18] (outside and inside, objective and subjective). How remarkably like the Tibetan, Kantian, Buberian, Marxian concepts noted above!

Lastly the Doctrine of the Mean envisions man honoring his virtuous nature by maintaining constant inquiry and study, seeking to carry it out to its "breadth and greatness," by "looking into the heart with perfect vision and acting." The key character entails man in action with ten pairs of eyes and one heart (mind).[19]

The Analects (Discourses and Dialogues between Confucius and Others) seem to have less to say on our theme, although there may be more than meets the eye. Legge considered them rather contemptuously as disconnected platitudes making little sense, but there are several interesting points, mainly as regards internal peace. Such will not be promoted by laws and punishments, but rather by virtuous example and the cultivation of a sense of shame.[20] Again, "when harmony prevails, there will be no scarcity of people" and "no rebellious upsettings" in states or families.[21] Most interesting is Confucius's reputed advice to Chi K'ang on the matter of "killing the unprincipled for the good of the principled." Confucius replied, "Sir, in carrying on your government, why should you use killing at all? Let your evinced desires be for what is good, and the people will be good. The relation between superiors and inferiors is like that between the wind and the grass. The grass must bend when the wind blows across it."[22]

The Great Learning (Ta Hsüeh) is a very brief work utilizing only seventy written characters. It might be put on a single page. All sorts of elaborate commentaries have been and may continue to be written on it. But its central message seems clear enough. It starts with things being investigated, which only man has the mind to do, proceeds through sincerity (or authenticity) in the description of them, and ends with "peace under Heaven."[23]Here again is the same message. Man has a mind; he uses it to study. When he sees things clearly enough and broadly enough, the desire (vision) for peace naturally emerges.

Taoism has some special contributions on the nature of the tranquil mind and the value of passivity (wu-wei)[24] but since it grew out of the same milieu as Confucianism we shall not dwell upon it, but shall skip across to some Western philosophy, though not to add examples of support for our proposition among idealists or pacifists. (Immanuel Kant, in his essay on "Perpetual Peace" [1795], speaks eloquently for these.)[25] Instead we shall seek some hope even in the tough-minded and cynical. Thus Plato is no pacifist. He urges having children watch warfare to acquire the stomach for it, and fighting foreigners with no holds barred, though he hopes that among Greeks there will be only civil wars, to improve society and not lay waste the land.[26]

Yet in *The Republic*, Socrates is asked whether we should censor violent acts from literature, poetry that plays on passions and the like. No, he says, but in primary education orderly things like music and mathmatics should be studied. Then the violence can be fed in and the student can keep it in perspective. It will be repugnant to the balanced (educated) person.[27]

Again, when Polemarchus defines justice as "helping friends and harming enemies," and Thrasymachus calls it "the interest of the stronger man," Socrates turns the whole thing upside down with his teacher-pupil and doctor-patient examples to show that the interest of any art of craft is the "interest" of the subject on which it is exercised.[28] To hurt him, or as in war, to kill him, is hardly the approach of a man who has straightened out his own thoughts and emotions.

Leaping to the twentieth century and Albert Camus violates my historian's chronological sensitivity, but "Les Justes" is his topic too, and philosophy is unbounded by time. Camus asks a more difficult question than any of Socrates' pupils. What is just treatment for the perpetrator of injustice and tyranny? Specifically, may he be killed? Yes, answers Camus, he may and should be bombed off the face of the earth—if he is not accompanied by innocent little children who would be killed or injured in the blast, and provided the killers for justice are prepared to die themselves.[29]

Does Camus desire peace, or does he desire revolutionary justice more? It seems to be the latter, until we reflect. He insists that the righteous killers die themselves, because having chosen to soar above their (human) race and pass judgment on it they are no longer fit to live as part of it. This would certainly limit the number of decisions to kill. But the other condition, no innocents killed, makes the proposition impossible. In killing the perpetrators of injustice little children and innocents are *always* present, usually right out in front.[30] There is actually no option. Hence we conclude that even the Camus of *Les Justes* desires peace.

L'Etat de siège* and *La Peste* are Camus's true war stories. Here is dramatized the kind of raw and mindless cruelty which the existentialists have shown up so well, and with examples of which they have rocked if not wrecked the lovely edifices of the Christian, Hegelian, Marxist, and presumably all other systematic explanations of human history. In *L'Etat*'s Cadiz all known manner of ruthlessness is let loose by the opportunity to kill townspeople by crossing out their names in the Secretary's notebook listing townspeople for death, as in a Hitlerian concentration camp or a selective conscription system. And in *La Peste*, symbolizing violence and hate, as the plague deaths mount the preacher can only say, "Maybe we should love that which we cannot understand," feeling is lost in body counts, and carriers of the disease are everywhere.

Yet in these also, as the horror wears itself out, two existentialist heroes stagger through. Diego tears up the notebook, and Dr. Rieux saves enough lives to begin anew, with a reaffirmation of the necessity for individual and existential attention to the plagues that threaten us.[31] Existentialism, it seems to me, far from negating the desire for peace seeks to place responsibility for keeping it on every individual, here and now, regardless of what the orders of the establishment say.

Hegel, of course, speaks for the establishment, the state, and is widely presumed to have opted for war, where the state does. The state possesses the Zeitgeist, spirit coming into time, the world mind manifested in its institutions, and he who does not have the same mind as the state is not free. Or whatever freedom he has is mere caprice or abstract freedom. He can't *do* anything unless he stays within the institutional embodiment of the spirit of the age (the state). But we should note that Hegel is the one philosopher who *is* concerned with time, that is, real historical time—chronological sequence. Thus the state *was* the embodiment of the world spirit of *his own* time (Georg Wilhelm Friedrich Hegel, 1770-1831) or at most the entire nineteenth century. Hegel had no delusions of immortality, for himself or the state. In the twentieth century the world spirit might very well be manifested in some other institutional arrangement, and if some would-be leader (like Hitler) tried to cling to the state too long, well, history would be the ultimate judge.[32]

History might even decide that the hippies manifest the Zeitgeist of the twentieth century, although their lack of institutional structure would stretch Hegel's system pretty far. The Untied Nations could definitely be a candidate, although it must be admitted that were Hegel alive today his admiration for bureaucracy would probably lead him to find the spirit in the American and

Soviet military-industrial complexes. Hegel did not desire peace in the concern-for-others-as-thyself sense of the more tender philosophies mentioned so far. But he did demand order within the best institutional framework of any given time, and a world-wide one wherein all could live in peace is certainly within the range of his philosophy.

Moreover, it is noteworthy that his disciple, Marx, also assumed to be an arch advocate of violence, was definitely not. Shlomo Avineri's recent studies make this crystal clear. Marx turned Hegel upside down and said that the spirit which came into the institutions of the time came, not down from on high but up from various social classes, and as the masses became aware, they would change things. This sounds and is revolutionary. However, it should be emphasized that Marx did not even advocate political conspiracy, much less violent revolution. He regarded the Jacobins as muddle-headed and their recourse to terrorism as merely proof that their aims could not be realized in their contemporary circumstances. Such activity as theirs, he argued, only radicalizes the dichotomy between the particularistic and the universal instead of producing a synthesis that incorporates and overcomes particularism. Society cannot be changed until people see the contradictions in their mode of life and want to change. No conspiracies are needed and any seeming need for violence merely shows that the effort is premature.[33] If Marx does not desire peace, at least he does not want war. He sees very clearly that social change through war is bound to be abortive.

We shall conclude this philosophical excursion with a return to Buddhism to ask why, if there is a desire for peace, is there such difficulty in attaining it? The problem seems to be in the relationship between knowing and acting. The superior man certainly knows what should be done, but does he know how to do it, and even knowing how to do it, does he do it? Of course he should, but he is also aware of the great damage done by inferior and mediocre men who, enmeshed in or still bothered by emotivity, wishfulness, and intellectual fog, go blithely about doing things wrongly and setting off ripples of error which may become tides of horror. Hence, he will be cautious.[34]

I am indebted to an excellent discourse on Zen Buddhism by Dr. Donald Swearer of Swarthmore College for the idea of an hourglass symbol.[35] In the beginning of his search, man-unknowing stands at the wide bottom of an hourglass, with his senses literally bombarded by the world around him. He makes no sense out of anything until he starts shutting things out and concentrating, meditating, narrowing his thoughts to the important ones. By so doing he rises to the neck of the hourglass, where suddenly enlightenment (*satori*) occurs, and he sees things as they are, without the I-Thou-It illusion. This, ideally, is his launching pad but he is so taken aback by the magnificence of the vision that he begins to act only slowly and tentatively; or he may not try to do anything but tell or teach what he has learned to a few others. Ultimately he can and should reenter all variety of everyday activities, which he will now more and more tend to accomplish correctly (without error), setting off ripples and then tides of compassion, love, and humanity.

The Tibetan sage Tsong-kha-pa (1357-1419) developed a special refinement in the technique of discovering when one is ready to act. Being completely certain intellectually that one has attained the "Real View" is not quite enough. One must search out every "scorpion"[36] of ego from every corner of one's psychological and emotional makeup. This can be accomplished by a progressing meditation of intensifying rigor focused first on one's mother, as the presumably most-loved object outside the ego. One meditates on her as the bestower of selfless mother-love, the pain she felt bringing one into the world, the care and feeding of one as an infant, with no thought of reward, and so on until for love of one's mother one "weeps uncontrollably and feels pain down to the roots of the hair." Then one transfers this feeling, step by step, to others dear to him, then less dear, then neutral, and so on to one's worst enemy, until one feels literally and absolutely that there is no difference between one's own beloved mother and one's worst enemy. Only then has one achieved "Complete Pure Realization"[37] of the "Real View" and may one begin to permit oneself to act.

Obviously most of us act all too soon; some, who have arrived at this state of intense compassionate feeling for others, may do too little too late. But in proper balance "the wind of compassion will blow across the grass" and even inferior men will learn shame, and peace.

We leave philosophy here, hopeful that we have made a case, not only for man's natural desire for peace, but with some hope for the realization of it.

Turning to history, we admit at once that it seems from the panoramic view to be one vast spectacle of violence and fireworks. But let us look at two general matters more closely. One was brought home to me by my colleague in the Conference on Peace Research in History, Professor Berenice Carroll of the University of Illinois, in her concluding essay for a volume of papers the conference is currently publishing. After remarking on "the almost unrecognized fact that peace really is the condition of life for most of humanity, over most of the globe, most of the time," she adds: "The statement that peace is the normal condition of human life is here affirmed as a conclusion of the author from her reading of history, from current research on wars since 1775, and from common-sense observations of life. The affirmation is probably correct, as the reader may agree upon a few moments of reflection. But it does not appear that any historian has troubled to demonstrate it, nor even to proclaim it as a fact."[38]

Secondly, as for the numerical count of the killing of human beings from the beginning of human history to the present, it is certainly very large. But if we break the figure into categories, the criminal (illegal) and the legal (or legalized), it seems quite certain that the legalized variety (legalized by war, courts, kangaroo courts, inquisitions, and the like) will far outnumber the former. Perhaps computers can give us the actual count some day.

From these two observations it would seem to be indicated that man has no natural desire to kill other human beings, that he must find rationalizations for doing so. Isn't the obverse of this "man's natural desire for peace"?

Then again we ask, from history this time, why is peace so elusive? Some twelve years ago I attempted a historical brainstorming session, the tentative results of which were published in a small and now forgottèn corner of the *American Historical Review.*[39] My purpose then was to try to get some of my professional colleagues to lift their eyes from their narrow fields of specialization to broader themes. They were too busy at that time, but let me try out some of the ideas here. Perhaps the Zeitgeist is coming in. Let us assume, as did Hegel, that there is a true, coherent, and explicable historical process at work in the world. What is it like? Is it Toynbee's challenge and response, or the rise and decay of civilizations? Is it competition for the world's resources, or for power? Religious struggle? Ideological struggle? I would suggest it is none of these. It is a story of man, with his unique mind, educating himself through the solution of interconnected problems, or rather problem sets. Where these problem sets came from we may not be able to answer, at least not until we solve the last segment of them, but they are with us and have been since the dawn of history. They may be described in four categories, in familiar terminology.

Problem set No. 1. "Physical science," from primitive agriculture to advanced engineering, medicine, and physics, including the economics of production. Cold, heat, hunger, and disease cause man discomfort. However, in the ground, sea, and air of this globe called Earth (and perhaps other planets) are resources which, if discovered and utilized, will enable him to attain material and physical well-being. These resources are hidden, some in easily discovered places (apples in trees), but others are literally embedded in illusions, oil in undèrground lakes in seemingly desolate areas, electricity in waterfalls, energy in atoms, and, of course, much more. The problem is their discovery and utilization. Not until recently (in historical terms) have anything but hit-or-miss methods been applied to the search, but gradually the realization that there are discoverable secrets of inestimable possibility has dawned, and men are organizing the search—amidst many distractions.

Problem set No. 2. "Social science," from primitive family and clan politics to world political systemizing, including economics of distribution. If men fight, they hurt each other and accomplish little, but if on the contrary they help each other, they can move forward much more rapidly to physical and material well-being. Hence the real object of politics is to keep from fighting. But why has it been so difficult? This is because there are several built-in illusions in the social as in the physical world—illusions which it has taken centuries for the broader intelligentsia (all mediocre men) even to identify, although a few prophets and sages, widely scattered in area and time, have had glimpses of insight, just as odd inventors have stumbled upon scientific discoveries. Such illusions include race, the idea that skin color is a real differential; and competition, the idea that one section of mankind can proper at the expense of another. Man has made some progress in solving these in in-groups of enlarging dimension, but he is just beginning to discover that the whole human race is in reality an in-group. The illusions are what make the problem, just as the fact that physical resources are hidden makes their discovery a problem.

Problem set No. 3. "Humanities," from child's play to great literature and art. The problem here is simply to discover the joy of living, though this is a subtle proposition. Whereas finding the way to physical and material well-being may constitute the serious business of the human race, the beauty of the world itself provides a first reminder to the observant that serious business should not be grim. And the fact that human difficulties and frailties can become joy in the theater suggests that the light touch, the arts in general, can and does serve as a kind of balm or lubricating oil in the working out of the serious problems.[40]

One need only consider these three problem sets in their interconnected way to see that they add up to a hope and a possibility not only for peace, but for general well-being and even pleasurable living.

There is a fourth set of problems, which I shall put under the general rubric "mental sciences." These include philosophy, psychology, and religion. (All of these, whether they derive ultimately from occult sources or not, must be treated by the historian as threads in the fabric of history.)

We have already shown that philosophy contains a positive answer to our query whether man has a natural desire for peace if he will use his mind to see things clearly. Of course, psychology has abundantly revealed man's baser side, the urges and the passions which complicate his educational process, but it should also be noted that the basic urges (as distinct from passions, which philosophy has shown how to neutralize) have a positive side too. Thus the urge to relieve discomfort propels man into the physical science problem set; the urge to reproduce necessitates his attention to that of the social sciences; and his urge to play (see Johan Huizinga, *Homo Ludens*)[41] brings on the humanities. Religion has, unhappily, been abundantly used to justify wars, particularly in the Western world with the Crusades, the jihad, the Thirty Years' War; but if the messages of brotherhood contained in the various warring religions were applied to all mankind instead of to the in-group of brethren controlling the symbols, idols, and sacred scripts, there can be no question of their voicing a desire for peace.

One haunting general question remains to be dealt with, the problem of the "animal nature" of humans, which is partly psychology, but is also biology. There can be no doubt that man is physically an animal. But in this paper we have avoided his animal linkage by stressing the capacity for development of his unique mind. The cynical will no doubt refuse to allow this loophole, and say that all we have proved is that man can be educated, or educate himself into a desire for peace, but that there is nothing "natural" about it. Darwin showed that the animal kingdom fights for survival, and the fittest survive. Man is an animal. But we have tried to show that as soon as man has neutralized the emotional, intellectual fog in which he is encompassed, seen through the illusions hiding his physical and social environment, and caught a glimpse of the "Real View" (the real reality) he will "naturally" desire peace, and will indeed go about obtaining it, by correct means. Only if we say that developing one's mind is not natural can we object to this, and it can certainly be argued that developing minds is as natural as developing muscles.

We have also suggested that the idea of evolution, which links man with lower animals, is the Western counterpart of the Eastern idea of reincarnation, which does the same thing. (This should bring us pause to question evolution a little more than we are accustomed to do; after all it is still only a theory.) At any rate evolution says nothing about the development of man's mind, which we repeat is unique.[42]

In addition, let us observe two points about the lower animals. One, which a young biologist called to my attention, is that animals rarely fight to the death, unless cornered. A dog will not further attack a dog which has rolled over in defeat, for instance.[43] Secondly, assuming the survival of the fittest theme, there is evidence that among animals those who cooperate best among themselves survive, not the biggest, strongest, and fiercest.[44] Perhaps, even in the animal kingdom there is a natural reluctance to kill?

In conclusion, let us take a close look at a specific historical problem in the real world of politics and diplomacy, and analyze its ingredients. It is not particularly important in historical annals, but it is relatively recent, as history goes, and it illustrates how and why the human mind should deal with real problems, not their shadows.

In 1887 the American planter element in Hawaii, which controlled the Hawaiian royal government behind the scenes, became alarmed at the potential political power of Japanese immigrants, whom they were bringing in by the thousands to work the plantations. They therefore compelled King Kalakaua to accept a constitution which gave foreign residents of American or European ancestry with certain property qualifications the right to vote and thereby control the legislature. By omission they excluded all Orientals.

The Japanese government immediately protested this as a violation of the existing treaty between Hawaii and Japan, which guaranteed Japanese subjects equal treatment with other foreign residents. There followed a long and dishonest exchange of letters between Hawaii and Japan, letters which illustrate very well how politicians and diplomats obscure the "Real View."

The Hawaiian foreign minister, an American named Austin, first told the Japanese that "hasty preparation" of the new constitution had resulted in an unintentional exclusion of Japanese from the suffrage, an exclusion "aimed solely at the Chinese." When the Japanese consul informed him that if the exclusion were indeed "unintentional" then, of course, it would be rectified shortly. Mr. Austin pointed out that since "the Asiatic subjects of Great Britain, Spain, Portugal, etc." were also excluded, there was really no discrimination against Japan. When the Japanese refused to accept this argument, he resorted to another, namely that since Japan did not grant her own subjects the right to vote at home, there certainly was no reason for them to have such a right in Hawaii.[45] To this the Japanese did not respond.

It should be noted that all this was taking place in a situation in which the American element had manipulated power away from the Hawaiian monarchy, which itself had sold out the rights of the Hawaiian people to foreigners. The Japanese, of course, were trying to edge in on a share of that doubly illegitimate power, which desire they later emphasized by sending warships "on a training cruise" to Hawaii. Yet desirous as they were of edging in on power in Hawaii, the Japanese leaders were unwilling to breathe a word about the possible right to vote of Japanese subjects in Japan, where a strong demand for it was already developing.

Also noteworthy is the cynical attempt by Mr. Austin to play on Japanese prejudice against the Chinese, and to utilize the presumptive "right" of Great Britain, Spain, Portugal, etc. to have Asiatic subjects who could not vote either at home or in Hawaii. All this from an American, who presumably would fight to the death for the Declaration of Independence, the Constitution of the United States, and Old Glory!

It is enough to turn a historian's stomach, especially that of one who is trying to show a desire for peace above power in the human race. However, happily or unhappily, the affair was smoothed over. Hawaii took the matter "under consideration" and later "under serious consideration," never doing anything. And Japanese leaders discovered they had more important things to do, like concocting a constitution which would prevent as many Japanese people from voting as possible. So, some "realist" historians would say, the processes of diplomacy worked their devious ways and war was averted.

But what would a "Real View" see? It would certainly see that in this little incident were encapsuled the elements of several of the sources of the troubles of the twentieth century: American expansion and racism; European colonialism; Japanese expansion, militarism, and oligarchy; Hawaiian, Chinese, and other Asian supineness in the face of discriminatory words and deeds.

But a "Real View" would also see that the situation was pregnant with opportunity for opening up some avenues of escape from the intellectual fog into which the principals had wandered. Americans should have seen that discriminatory practices against Asians were going to sow the seeds of hatred and discord with people of that vast continent; the Japanese should have seen that Japan could hardly expect her citizens to be treated well abroad while they were herded like cattle at home; both should have seen that European colonialism was a poison to be eliminated rather than utilized to condone further malpractices; and Hawaiians, Chinese, and other Asians should have gone on a sitdown strike until some honest facing of these issues came forth. Hawaii might have emerged as a real model of a Nirvana of the future instead of a future site of Pearl Harbor. It should be noted in passing that two "radicals" of the time had glimpses of these realities, one Walter Murray Gibson and one Robert W. Wilcox. Both were arrested, with Gibson allowed to take ship and flee to San Francisco, and Wilcox later tried for treason, though acquitted by a Hawaiian jury. [46]

Confucius said: "The superior man bends his attention to that which is radical. That being established, all practical courses naturally grow up." [47]

—5—

Power and Peace

G. Warren Nutter

The scholar is constantly frustrated and embarrassed, a revered mentor of mine used to say, by finding it necessary to prove that water runs downhill. I feel that way today as I speak to a subject best addressed by history: the role of power in keeping the peace. Yet the message of history is often unlearned, and I will not apologize for repeating it familiar as it may be, from my point of view.

We have come to one of those times in which many earnest citizens set all things military on one side and peace on the other. Since war is waged by the military, they conclude that peace will be achieved only when the military disappears. What, aside from logic, is wrong with this line of reasoning?

First, we should take a look at what we mean by peace. Perhaps the only thing more difficult than maintaining peace is defining it. But we need not be concerned with philosophical niceties here, for the basic problem before us is one of relations among nations. Of course, nations are at peace in the trite sense when they are not in combat. In a more fundamental sense, they are at peace when some are not threatening to use open force against others in order to alter the existing order of things, either within or among them.

To go much farther in defining peace would rob the word of content and relevance. It would be utopian, for instance, to describe peace as a state of affairs in which all parties are satisfied with the status quo, or to equate peace with universal bliss, or with the absence of implicit threats of violence. Men and nations being what they are, there will always be conflicts of interest of all sorts, and the important question is how they will be resolved, whether through coercion or agreement.

What makes nations choose the path of violence? Why does one nation go to war against another? One could obviously catalogue many reasons, and I would not presume to lecture on them before an institution celebrating its golden anniversary of inquiry into this arcane subject. I will instead focus on one specific condition that has characterized much of history.

Let there be a powerful nation, and let it be governed by whatever group holds the reins of power. Let those in power be determined, for one reason or another, to change the state of affairs in the surrounding world; in a word, be

64

committed to altering the accepted status quo in other societies. The stage is then obviously set for conquest and violence.

Violence need not ensue, of course, if the threatened nations do not value the prevailing culture enough to fight for it. It need not ensue for two other reasons: because the threatened nations are too weak to resist, or because they are too strong to be attacked. The only difference in the last two cases is the outcome. In both cases there is no war, but in the one there is conquest and in the other repulse. That is the sole difference.

For this characterization to make sense, the nations in question obviously must not be mutually threatening one another. Such a situation is not unknown, but we are not discussing it now. We are instead talking about one nation or group of nations that is minding its own business without harming anyone else, and another that is aggressively meddling.

This is surely not to say that the peaceful nations are, if we may speak of their collective mentalities, fully satisfied with the existing state of affairs either within or beyond their boundaries. Quite the contrary is normally the case. The difference comes in the means used, first, to decide on desirable change, and second, to effect it.

We now come straight to the issue of deterrent power. A deterrent is relevant only if there is a deterree, or somebody who must be discouraged or restrained from committing forceful harm. Just as beauty is in the eye of the beholder, so also is deterrence in the mind of the deterree.

A story is told of an ancient Chinese strategist whose skills were legendary. The enemy mounted a large force against him and marched upon the citadel that formed the strongpoint of his defenses. Unfortunately, he had dispatched his troops to another field of battle and found himself undefended as the hordes gathered to attack. Sizing up the situation quickly, he ordered the gates of the citadel thrown open and a large banquet spread upon the ramparts. As the enemy approached, he sat majestically at the table, partaking of the feast and beckoning the enemy to enter the gates. Mindful of his genius, the attacking generals would not believe what their eyes told them. They saw no defenders on the battlements or within the city, but they were not to be so easily deceived. Taking counsel, they quickly decided that an attack was doomed to failure, and so they withdrew.

We cannot, of course, carry the moral of this story too far, but it illustrates, through an extreme example, the point being made. If the enemy bent on attack is to be deterred, he must assess in his own mind that the party he threatens is both able and willing to deliver a crippling blow. Manifest power need not be employed openly to be effective.

This principle applies equally to nations that threaten others. There is no need to engage in violence as long as the threat to do so will work as well. Diplomacy is therefore a useful instrument of power politics.

It is surely correct that the antithesis of conflict is rational discourse with the view to resolving problems through voluntary agreement. This is what we mean when we speak of government by discussion. Yet we must be careful to recognize that bargaining, negotiating, and compromising often go beyond the bounds of rational discourse among friends bent on reaching peaceful consensus, particularly in the area of international diplomacy.

Given the international scene we have postulated, with some nations determined to change the existing state of affairs, we cannot expect that agreements will be reached at the negotiating table solely on the basis of logic, reason, and persuasion. The threat of force stands waiting in the wings, just visible to the negotiating parties. Leaders of a powerful country determined to have their way will not be satisfied with resting their case on its intellectual, historical, and ethical merits. They will be prepared to do more than offer inducements and concessions of one kind or another to achieve their basic goals. They will not shrink from the threat, implicit or explicit, or forcibly denying legitimate rights or of imposing harmful consequences.

Those nations innocent of designs on others and desirous of settling international problems without coercion must face this reality. If they renounce military strength, as their instincts urge, they place themselves at the mercy of aggressors at the negotiating table as well as on the battlefield. Indeed, the one is merely another form of the other. The innocent nations must have sufficient armed strength to deter the use of aggressive force in either case.

One hardly needs to be reminded that this is a sorry and tragic state of affairs. How much more desirable it would be if goodwill and peaceful intent prevailed everywhere. But does it make sense for a lamb to bargain with a wolf? President Nixon drove this point home in his speech before the Air Force Academy in June 1969, when he said:

> ... there is one school of thought that holds that the road to understanding with the Soviet Union and Communist China lies through a downgrading of our own alliances and what amounts to a unilateral reduction of our own arms—in order to demonstrate our good faith.
>
> They believe that we can be conciliatory and accommodating only if we do not have the strength to be otherwise, they believe Americans will be able to deal with the possibility of peace only when we are unable to cope with the threat of war.
>
> Those who think that way have grown weary of the weight of free world leadership that fell upon us in the wake of World War II. They argue that we, the United States, are as much responsible for the tension in the world as the adversary we face.

Nations can negotiate on many things, including limits on their respective armed power. We face the paradox, however, that a nation must be strong before it can negotiate with a powerful antagonist on mutual reduction of strength.

Having all this in mind, we need to be clear about one thing: confrontation is always to be avoided in favor of meaningful negotiations, whenever the choice is open. Wise diplomacy on the part of a reasonable government, when backed by sufficient strength, offers far more hope for peaceful resolution of problems than a policy of unyielding confrontation.

But we must not expect too much of diplomacy. In particular, we must guard against the illusion that a stable pattern of relations, once successfully negotiated from properly balanced strength, will endure forever. If nothing else, relative power changes over time, destabilizing the initial order. We need look no farther than the tragic interwar period in Europe and Asia to draw this lesson. As has been so often noted, the problem is one of continually balancing power rather than achieving a balance. In mapping foreign policy based on negotiation, one must keep a step ahead of the times to be successful in the deeper sense.

The dynamic demands of international politics can easily lead to frustration, and frustration in turn to the urge to withdraw. Thence flows the philosophy of the Maginot Line or Fortress America, which is even less relevant to changing conditions than the worst international order it is designed to replace. Here is a case of excessive reliance on a particular variety of strength: defensive, passive, and inflexible. It can succeed only if every powerful nation retreats into its own fortress, a situation hardly consistent with the reasons for withdrawal in the first place.

How, then, does a country of peaceful intent make its way through the maze of world politics? How does it protect its own legitimate interests when it must reckon with hostile designs on the part of other nations of varying identity and power?

It makes sure, first of all, that it has sufficient strength and resolution to cope with the rigors of world politics. It seeks, secondly, the path of negotiation as far as other nations will go along. And it prepares itself, finally, to deter and, if necessary, to repulse hostilities. To neglect any one of these elements of foreign policy is to invite disaster.

As I speak today, negotiators from the United States and the Soviet Union are gathered in Helsinki for preliminary talks on how we can curb the nuclear arms race. No negotiations in recent times have been more critical, and we in your government are determined to pursue them seriously, soberly, and realistically, with the objective of reaching a successful outcome. To do so, we must fully appreciate the realities of power confronting us. Let me give you some of the specifics, already reviewed in many public forums but perhaps worth repeating.

As we come to the bargaining table, we find that the Soviets are continuing a rapid buildup of strategic forces that seems to reach beyond their defensive needs and presents a potential menace to our own deterrent of nuclear warfare. I speak here not of surmise or speculation on our part, but of simple fact. It is a simple and unassailable fact, attested by hard evidence, that the Soviet Union is extending its deployment of the SS-9 intercontinental ballistic missile. This enormous missile is capable of delivering a 25-megaton warhead, and possibly could carry three separate 5-megaton warheads.

Reflect if you will on the destructive power of such a weapon. A 25-megaton warhead is twelve hundred and fifty times as powerful as the atomic weapon released on Hiroshima. What possible need is there for such a weapon in the arsenal of deterrence? The only prudent assumption is that it could be designed to destroy our retaliatory Minuteman missile in its hardened silo.

Simultaneously, the Soviet Union is expanding its Polaris-type submarine fleet at the rate of seven or eight submarines a year, and that rate could be accelerated on the basis of installed capacity. This development could threaten the safety of our strategic bombing force if it were to be caught on the ground.

We cannot of course know what Soviet leaders intend to do, but we can appreciate what they are capable of doing. And it is the responsibility of the Defense Department to guard against the capabilities of an adversary. In fulfilling this responsibility, we cannot blink the fact that, if the present Soviet weapons buildup continues at its current pace, and if improvements are made that are already technically feasible, our strategic deterrent and retaliatory force could be in jeopardy by the mid 1970s.

As Secretary Laird has emphasized, the Defense Department would be gambling irresponsibly with our nation's security if it were to assume that Soviet leaders have no intention of using the capability they are now developing. I am confident that the American public agrees with the Secretary. We all recall the peril of the Cuban missile crisis in 1962, when this country was caught by surprise. Up to the very time photographic evidence demonstrated that Soviet offensive missiles were installed in Cuba, it was widely assumed that the Soviet Union had no such intentions.

The Defense Department will focus on the capabilities rather than the intentions of the enemy, first, to do everything possible to avoid a similar crisis in the future, and second, to ensure that we are able to cope with one if it should nevertheless arise. We mastered the Cuban crisis because we had a credible deterrent. It is sobering to reflect on what the outcome could otherwise have been.

Let me be absolutely clear on one point: there is no doubt that we have a credible deterrent today. That point is not at issue. What is at issue is whether we maintain that deterrent unimpaired—not today, not tomorrow, but in the period beginning in the mid 1970s. What is at issue, too, is whether we discourage efforts to erode the credibility of our deterrent by demonstrating our will and ability to maintain it.

If we take no countering action now and simply permit our Minuteman missiles and strategic bombers to become vulnerable, the credibility of our deterrent would be diminished with serious consequences for our national security and our hopes for peace.

In preparing our defenses, we must think ahead for two reasons: first, because technological progress moves at a rapid pace; and, second, because complex weapons often require as long as five to ten years of development before becoming operational. Our defensive posture of the mid 1970s and beyond depends on decisions made now.

Let me be more specific. If we did not respond to the developing threat, we might have to place all our eggs in the Polaris basket. To rely solely on the Polaris/Poseidon weapon system, however much confidence we now have in its survivability and effectiveness, would be to run an unacceptable risk. The problem confronting an adversary who contemplated an attack against us would be greatly simplified, and he would be tempted to develop a first-strike capability against us. The effectiveness of our diplomatic policies would be undermined and crises would become increasingly unstable. The adversary might believe that he could significantly reduce damage to his homeland in a nuclear exchange by striking first against our land-based forces.

For all of these reasons, our government has consistently appreciated the wisdom of maintaining an independent retaliatory capability in each component of its nuclear forces—missiles, strategic bombers, and submarines.

This balanced mixture of strategic forces ensures protection of our national security in three ways. First, it provides us with insurance of an effective military capability in the event that one or two of the major components of the system should be neutralized by the enemy. Second, it confronts the enemy with the need to divert resources from offensive uses to complex defensive needs. Third, it reduces the risk that technological advances not now clearly foreseen may degrade our deterrent.

Very early in its tenure, the Nixon Administration confronted the issue posed by the Soviet threat to our deterrent. Alternative systems for countering this threat were carefully analyzed in accord with four basic requirements:

1. The system must be effective.
2. It must be relatively inexpensive.
3. It must not stimulate an arms race.
4. It must not disrupt the prospects for negotiations on limitation of strategic arms.

The Safeguard ABM system, designed to protect our bombers and missile sites from attack, best fulfilled all these requirements.

First, tests have shown it to be effective in the use for which it is designed.

Second, it is less expensive than any alternative system, involving an outlay of less than $1 billion in fiscal 1970 and a maximum of $6 to $7 billion if full deployment becomes necessary over a stretched-out period. I don't want to suggest for a moment that these resources could not achieve a great deal of good on the domestic front, but we must place this one-time expenditure in the proper perspective. The prudence of paying a relatively modest insurance premium to safeguard the wealth and safety of our nation seems obvious, particularly when we recognize that we spend about $22 billion every year on procurement of arms and equipment.

Third, the purely defensive posture of the Safeguard system provides no cause to the Soviet Union to escalate the arms race unless it really intends to attain the means to destroy our land-based retaliatory forces. In that case there is all the more reason for us to take this defensive action at once.

Fourth, for the same reason, this program does not damage the prospects for arms talks. Moreover, the flexible and time-phased nature of Safeguard makes it possible for us to alter our deployment at any stage consistent with progress in negotiations.

Keep in mind that the Safeguard system calls for installation of antiballistic missiles around our Minuteman sites and strategic bomber bases, not around our cities.

The Safeguard system also provides an option for protecting our population against a light attack by intercontinental ballistic missiles such as one that Communist China will probably be capable of launching in the 1970s. In addition, it affords a means of defense against the accidental firing of a missile by any power.

There were some who argued that we should not proceed with Safeguard because, among other reasons, the Soviets would misinterpret our intentions and consequently reject our invitation to engage in the Strategic Arms Limitation Treaty discussions. This prediction has been proven wrong.

Safeguard is a purely defensive move on our part, a move essential for the cause of peace at this historical juncture. We cannot allow our deterrent to erode while we are in the very process of negotiating means for curbing the arms race.

Our hopes for peace and our desire to build a better America may lead some to disregard the international arena and the challenges to our very existence that we face there. Those same hopes and desires may also lead some to conclude that we should sharply and immediately diminish the burdens of our national defense.

It is because I have those hopes and desires that I cannot agree with these conclusions. Together with Secretary Laird, I have pledged all my effort to the true mission of the Department of Defense: restoration and preservation of peace and tranquility. If we do not weaken in our resolve to achieve this goal now that it may not be too far from our grasp, we can look forward to early fulfillment of our desire to build a better America. If we do otherwise, we might have no America to build.

—6—

Technology and Peace:
The Role of Biological Research

Joshua Lederberg

I. INTRODUCTION

My original assignment was to comment broadly on the subject of my title. To fulfill it properly, however, was beyond the scope of the allotted time and space. For a detailed analysis of the role of biological research on peace, I should have had to consider at least the following topics:

First, the evolution and biology of man as a foundation for personal and organized conflict, comprising the interrelationships among inherited instincts (and their diversity among individuals); the transmission and mutation of tradition from one generation to the next; the forms of global political organization; and the diagnosis and treatment of human failings from a biological, psychological, and sociocultural standpoint.

Second, the modernization of aspiring countries and peoples, including the improvement of crops, which has a strong base in biotechnology but so far has had only a minimal infusion of the most recent advances in molecular biology; the conservation of human capital, that is, public health, with particular emphasis on the impact of malnutrition on the development of intellectual and moral vigor; the development of the world's agricultural economy to the level of its industrial economy, with concern for the shocks of technological displacement (for example, what if a satisfactory, cheap synthetic substitute for coffee were discovered?); and improved techniques for controlling the rate of population growth within the capital resources of a country and within the carrying capacity of the earth.

Third, the protection of the global environment.

This inquiry is obviously too broad for proper treatment here. I have therefore refined my topic to the threat of biological warfare, which is undoubtedly the most fearful biological threat to peace.

The remarks in part II are presented substantially as delivered at the conference on November 18, 1969.[1] A few days later, they were (happily) mooted in some measure by President Nixon's announcement on November 25 unilaterally

71

renouncing U.S. capabilities for biological warfare. [2] In part III, I offer some current afterthoughts (as of April 1970) concerning further steps that have yet to be taken for the bolstering of biological science as an instrument of peaceful change and well-being.

II. BIOLOGICAL WARFARE AND THE EXTINCTION OF MAN

I am grateful for this opportunity to express my profound concern about the continued involvement of this and other nations in the development of biological warfare. This process has put the very future of human life on earth in serious peril. It is all the more tragic because the great powers who should be hastening to institute international controls have little to gain and much to lose in relation to the present balance of nuclear deterrence. A serious side effect of biological warfare work by the major powers is the inevitable proliferation of a destabilizing strategic capacity for preemptive attack and for clandestine harassment.

Chemical warfare, though well demonstrated at a tactical level, is less important strategically, and is complicated by many technical details. Furthermore, it lacks the special hazard of contagion which makes biological warfare a unique peril to world peace.

Our ratification of the Geneva Protocol of 1925 would represent only the first small step toward the negotiation of international controls. However, so long as we have isolated ourselves as the only major power to refuse to enter this commitment, there is little chance for further negotiation. It leaves on record a low and unconvincing reading, indeed, of our earnestness as a nation in seeking world order for the management of this problem.

My own research career has centered on the genetics of bacteria. With Dr. E. L. Tatum, then at Yale, I had the thrill of discovering genetic recombination in bacteria. Later at the University of Wisconsin with my then graduate student Norton Zinder (like E. L. Tatum now a professor at Rockefeller University), I was privileged to help unearth genetic transduction (the use of viruses to convey information from cell to cell). I have also studied bacterial mutation, for example to resistance against the action of antibiotic drugs, in work that complemented the pioneering studies of Drs. S. E. Luria and Max Delbrück, who were named for the 1969 Nobel Prize in medicine.

Basic scientists who have worked in the genetics of bacteria and viruses believe that these discoveries have ever-growing importance for the prevention and healing of serious human diseases. In the present era, we live in incompletely justified optimism about having "conquered infectious bacterial disease" through the development of antibiotics. But viruses are, in general, still beyond the reach of antibiotic therapy. Even bacteria, believed to be under firm control with antibiotics, are evolving and continuing their assaults upon human health with renewed vigor. In the long run, only our continued vigilance over bacterial evolution can justify our hope of maintaining a decisive lead in this life-and-death race.

Whatever pride I might wish to take in the eventual human benefits that may arise from my own research, however, is turned into ashes by the application of this kind of scientific insight to the engineering of biological warfare agents. We are in somewhat the same position as the nuclear physicists who foresaw the development of atomic weapons.

There is, however, a crucial difference. Nuclear weaponry depends on the most advanced industrial technology, and it has been monopolized by the great powers long enough to sustain a de facto balance of deterrence and to build a security system based on nonproliferation. Nuclear power has thus, ironically, become a stabilizing factor tending to reinforce the status quo parallel to established levels of economic and industrial development. Germ power will work just the other way.

The United Nations Study Report on chemical and biological weaponry has summarized some infectious agents that have served as points of departure for the development of biological weapons. Any knowledgeable virologist could suggest many more. I will not repeat these technical details, nor will I bludgeon you with the horrible diseases some of these agents provoke. I will also leave to your own conscience the burden of moral judgment about using these weapons. Most Americans would be repelled by the thought, but perhaps no less than by exposure to the human realities of any other form of warfare. Overriding such comparisons should be the grave moral issue of a policy that risks the lives of a world of innocent bystanders. Fortunately, these concerns actually converge with our self-interest in calling a halt to biological warfare before it becomes established in the arms traffic of the world.

My main fears about biological warfare have to do with the side effects of its proliferation: as a technique of aggression of small nations and insurgent groups, and the inadvertent spread of disease.

If the great powers could actually protect the secrecy of their biological warfare work I would be much less alarmed. The chance of biological warfare ever being used in a major strategic attack is essentially negligible in the face of the nuclear deterrent. The suggestion that we need biological or chemical warfare weapons for specific retaliatory purposes in order to deter their use aims at a ridiculous kind of precision. Will our deterrent missiles have to follow the same trajectories as those that might potentially attack us? Will they have to be launched at the same time of day? Will they have to have the same mix of explosive energy and radioactive fallout? If we are attacked with anthrax strain B27 must we reply with anthrax B27?

On the other hand, if I were a Machiavellian adviser to a would-be Hitler I might indeed advocate a considerable investment in biological weaponry as a desperate approach to the cheap acquisition of great power even if at very great risk. And, of course, the first thing I would do would be to plant my intelligence agents in the existing biological warfare establishments of the high-budget powers in order to get the necessary scientific information at the lowest possible cost.

However, if I were patient I would not bother to do even that. No security system, no counterintelligence system in the world expects a delay of more than five to ten years in the leakage of vital information. We do not have, and I presume do not contemplate, a security reservation like wartime Los Alamos for the containment of biological warfare research. If a high level of activity is to be maintained there will be frequent turnover of personnel. It is unreasonable to expect a tighter security barrier here than has prevailed in any other area, given the problems of reconciling security with a free society. Besides these channels for diffusion of information, there are also bound to be *Pueblo*-like incidents, and calculated leaks in the budget competition of the services. The American people might be the last to know; but we can rely on hardly more than a ten-year delay between many important discoveries in biological warfare research laboratories and their availability to hostile and irresponsible forces outside.

As a matter of prudent self-protection, biological warfare research laboratories in the United States and the United Kingdom have pioneered in the technology of containing dangerous microbes. I have great respect for the technical capabilities of the senior civilian management of these laboratories. They should be credited with the utmost diligence in protecting both their personnel and the surrounding communities. They have also published a great deal of their work in the engineering of such protective facilities, and this experience is unquestionably of great value in public health work. For example, the British laboratories at Porton were acclaimed for the safe handling of the very dangerous Marburg virus upon its first outbreak in Europe two years ago.

In spite of these precautions, disease organisms have nevertheless escaped from time to time, and inevitably will do so in the future. Such escapes already constitute a breach of security. They also compromise public health, which is further threatened by keeping civilian physicians in ignorance of potential agents that might explode into large-scale epidemics. The intentional development of virulent strains resistant to conventional antibiotics obviously worsens the problem. We simply have no way of assuring that a biological warfare development will not eventually seed a catastrophic worldwide epidemic that ignores national boundaries.

On the immediate horizon are modern developments in molecular genetics. These undoubtedly point to the development of agents against which no reasonable defense can be mounted. Because of the uncertain danger of retroaction, such agents are hardly likely to be used as a result of any rational military decision, but would obviously play into the hands of aggressive insurgence and blackmail. Finally, even the publication, albeit as a positive contribution to humanity, of the technology of safe containment insidiously helps solve a problem that might have hindered a potential insurgent from dabbling in biological warfare.

The problem of containing infectious agents being manufactured and stockpiled in large quantities, or tested in the open air, is a much more difficult technological challenge; and it is encumbered with even more official secrecy than the laboratory work. We have the Skull Valley incident to help judge the competence with which such matters might be handled. The main effect of security has not been to deny information to an enemy but to protect an establishment from both destructive and constructive criticism at home. In this case, more open constructive criticism would be crucial for assurance that procedures for containing microbes are well conceived and correctly implemented.

Biological warfare agents for use against man can be expected to be far more capricious than any other form of weapon. For any strategic purpose they are essentially untestable since large populations would have to be held to an uncertain risk. With nuclear weapons we can at least be confident of the laws of scaling. The destruction of targets can be calculated from simple physical measurements like the energy released. Nothing comparable to this can possibly apply to biological warfare agents. For this reason, again, the United States and other nuclear powers have absolutely nothing to lose in disavowing their use in war. Our continued participation in biological warfare development is akin to our arranging to make hydrogen bombs available at the supermarket.

Microbiological research must be expanded in programs of public health research for defense against our natural enemies. But the public health bureaucracy has refused to give prudent thought to the recurrence of major pandemics of human disease, be they of spontaneous or human-intelligent origin; perhaps this is simply a consequence of their sense of futility about mobilizing the necessary measure of global health needed to protect the species. If we add to already urgent concerns the spread of dangerous diseases from large foci of infection established by biological warfare attack, the prospects become even gloomier.

Our self-interest both as Americans and human beings urgently calls for the institution of improved measures of world public health and of international controls on the development and use of biological warfare agents. Research related to biological warfare should perhaps continue; but it is of the first importance that this be fear-reducing rather than fear-generating, for the latter can only lead to mutual escalation of antihuman developments.

It is difficult at this stage to detail the character of new agreements subsequent to our ratifications of the Geneva Protocol. We cannot suddenly impose unilateral decisions on the international community; but no other issue can evoke such a unanimity of world opinion. New agreements probably should include (1) public legal commitments against secret biological warfare research; (2) the establishment of central, international laboratories to monitor the occurrence of threatening organisms and to help develop generally available means of protection against them; (3) a legal system to protect the freedom of information and communication of data on disease organisms to such central authorities; (4) a general acceleration of research and health services to minimize the incidence of infectious disease, particularly in underdeveloped countries. No situation could be better designed for the evolution of serious new viruses than the existence of crowded, underfed human populations in which foci could develop and spread with a minimum of medical control; (5) treaty commitments on biological warfare analogous to the nuclear nonproliferation treaty; (6) pre-agreed sanctions by the civilized world against the release or development of biological warfare agents, clearly invoking international law against such "offenses against mankind" as akin to war crimes.

Some of the possibilities I have outlined are speculations which I fervently hope will be proven false. Unfortunately, they already have a proven historical precedent. As many of you already know, the Black Death—the epidemic of bubonic plague in Europe between 1347 and 1350—was the immediate consequence of a primitive form of bacteriological warfare. Genoese colonists in the Crimea brought the plague back to Italy with them when they retreated from the fortress of Feodosiya after having been assaulted with the corpses of the attacking Tatar hordes who had been infested with the disease. This epidemic subsided only after killing approximately one third of the population of Europe, as well, presumably, as taking an equal toll in Asia and India. Unless we learn to apply our common energies against the common enemies of all mankind, we are foolish and arrogant to doubt that history will record Black Death II, and more.

III. POSTSCRIPT (APRIL 1970)

President Nixon's announcement of November 25, 1969 (see Appendix I) was a major turning point in United States policy on biological warfare. At the very least it has relieved the prospect that American scientific ingenuity would be actively addressed to the development of these dangerous weapons. Until effective international agreements are negotiated and adopted, the danger remains that other countries will persevere in such development; however, most of their motive for doing so will have evaporated by virtue of our own abrogation. Furthermore, such countries have less highly developed scientific and technological expertise for basic innovations in microbiology, although they are well equipped to exploit advances that might be initiated here. These would inevitably "leak" in the course of time despite the most strenuous efforts to maintain their secrecy.

It is deplorable and discouraging that this unilateral step has not been followed by similar renunciations by Soviet bloc countries, which have voiced the loudest complaints about our own previous neglect of biological warfare issues.[3] In part this may be a bargaining move in an effort to push U.S. negotiators at the disarmament conferences into more comprehensive commitments than they have so far been able to agree to for want of reliable methods of verification. In part, this lack of response may also relate to the uncertainty of the exact meaning and intended implementation of the President's policy statement.

For example, suppose the Soviet Union were also to state that it would now "confine its biological research to defensive measures," if indeed it has not done so long since. Might we not assume that this language blanketed the same range of activities as prevailed beforehand? After all, no nation labels its military establishment as a Department of Offense!

In fact, the political realities of this country insure that Mr. Nixon's intentions go far beyond semantic games; and they may be expressed soon in such drastic measures as the piecemeal abandonment of the biological warfare research centers at Fort Detrick, and Pine Bluff, Arkansas. This is unfortunate, for these facilities are valuable resources in physical plant and in organized manpower for which other vital tasks are pressing. For example, Fort Detrick might be reclaimed as an *international* center for epidemic diseases, including biological warfare defense as one aspect of its open research program. The step-by-step implementation of Mr. Nixon's announcement will, I fear, dull most of the impact it could have on a suspicious world were its operational scope to be outlined in advance.

On the diplomatic front, the United States has joined the United Kingdom in proposals to deal with biological weapons promptly and separately from chemical weapons (see Appendix II). The technical arguments for distinguishing these are well stated by Ambassador Gerard Smith, and I would support this endeavor to complete a formal convention to abolish biological warfare as a first step. In effect, secrecy for any government research on agents of disease must (and ought to) be eliminated.

The problems of verification, even of definition, of a capability in chemical weaponry are much more serious. During the early stages of international rapprochement, unilateral initiatives (amounting to implicit negotiation) may be the most effective—a supposition that would be more plausible were there more evidence of a response to the first gambit on biological weapons.

It would help in the control of chemical warfare to organize a U.N. consultative group to identify toxic compounds with chemical warfare potential and devoid of peaceful uses. The U.N. group could then seek a registration of the compounds thus labeled and publish an accounting of their distribution. The United Nations should also provide technical facilities for the detection of chemical and biological warfare attack, and for the investigation of complaints concerning incidents involving these weapons.

In the long run, it is the will of the great powers that will decide the further evolution of this issue. If peace and stability is their shared aim, the powers will discourage desperate experiments with these tools. If they are more preoccupied with stirring up trouble for each other, they will encourage chemical warfare capabilities within their spheres of influence. Is it to our interest, or to the Soviets', to forfend nuclear proliferation only to have it replaced by equi-lethal chemicals?

APPENDIX I

STATEMENT BY PRESIDENT RICHARD M. NIXON, ANNOUNCING POLICY DECISIONS ON CHEMICAL AND BIOLOGICAL WARFARE PROGRAMS ON NOVEMBER 25, 1969

Soon after taking office I directed a comprehensive study of our chemical and biological defense policies and programs. There has been no such review in over fifteen years. As a result, objectives and policies in this field were unclear and programs lacked definition and direction.

Under the auspices of the National Security Council, the Departments of State and Defense, the Arms Control and Disarmament Agency, the Office of Science and Technology, the Intelligence Community and other agencies worked closely together on this study for over six months. These government efforts were aided by contributions from the scientific community through the President's Scientific Advisory Committee.

This study has now been completed and its findings carefully considered by the National Security Council. I am now reporting the decisions taken on the basis of this review.

Chemical Warfare Program

As to our chemical warfare program, the United States:

— Reaffirms its oft-repeated renunciation of the first use of lethal chemical weapons.

— Extends this renunciation to the first use of incapacitating chemicals.

Consonant with these decisions, the Administration will submit to the Senate, for its advice and consent to ratification, the Geneva Protocol of 1925 which prohibits the first use in war of "asphyxiating, poisonous or other Gases and of Bacteriological Methods of Warfare." The United States has long supported the principles and objectives of this Protocol. We take this step toward formal ratification to reinforce our continuing advocacy of international constraints on the use of these weapons.

79

Biological Research Program

Biological weapons have massive, unpredictable and potentially uncontrollable consequences. They may produce global epidemics and impair the health of future generations. I have therefore decided that:

> The U.S. shall renounce the use of lethal biological agents and weapons, and all other methods of biological warfare.

> The U.S. will confine its biological research to defensive measures such as immunization and safety measures.

> The DOD has been asked to make recommendations as to the disposal of existing stocks of bacteriological weapons.

In the spirit of these decisions, the United States associates itself with the principles and objectives of the United Kingdom Draft Convention which would ban the use of Biological methods of warfare. We will seek, however, to clarify specific provisions of the draft to assure that necessary safeguards are included.

Neither our association with the Convention nor the limiting of our program to research will leave us vulnerable to surprise by an enemy who does not observe these rational restraints. Our intelligence community will continue to watch carefully the nature and extent of the biological programs of others.

These important decisions, which have been announced today, have been taken as an initiative toward peace. Mankind already carries in its own hands too many of the seeds of its own destruction. By the examples we set today, we hope to contribute to an atmosphere of peace and understanding between nations and among men.

APPENDIX II

STATEMENT OF AMBASSADOR GERARD SMITH, DIRECTOR
U.S. ARMS CONTROL AND DISARMAMENT AGENCY
AT THE CONFERENCE OF THE COMMITTEE
ON DISARMAMENT (CCD), GENEVA
FEBRUARY 6, 1970

Regarding biological weapons, President Nixon stated that the United States renounces the use of all biological weapons; that the United States will confine its biological research to defensive measures such as immunization and safety and that plans will be prepared for the disposal of existing stocks of biological weapons. The President also stated that in the spirit of these decisions, the United States associates itself with the principles and objectives of the United Kingdom Draft Convention which would ban biological methods of warfare.

Underlining his support for the United Kingdom convention, President Nixon announced on February 15 that the United States also renounces preparations for and the use of toxins as a method of warfare, and that it will confine its military program for toxins, whether produced by bacteriological or other biological methods or by chemical synthesis, to research for defensive purposes only. The President further directed the destruction of all existing toxin weapons.

In announcing his decisions regarding U. S. chemical and biological programs, President Nixon remarked that we had tried "to find the facts and to develop the policies based on the facts as they are, rather than on our fears as to what the facts might be." There are significant differences between the properties and potential military utility of chemical and biological weapons which indicate the desirability of treating them separately in the context of arms control negotiations. Chemical weapons are primarily tactical weapons; biological weapons are principally a strategic threat to large areas and to large population concentrations. Moreover, chemical weapons have been used in warfare and a number of countries have a chemical warfare capability or are conducting research in this field. A number of these states maintain chemical warfare programs to deter the use against them of chemical warfare and to provide a retaliatory capability if deterrence fails. I believe they would be reluctant to give up this capability unless they were assured that all possible opponents had also given it up and would not again develop it. Such assurance would be difficult to achieve even with very extensive inspections. Biological weapons on the other hand have never been used and few nations appear to have engaged in substantial effort to develop biological warfare. It is in light of these facts that we believe a comprehensive ban on biological warfare should be feasible at this time but that an agreement for a joint ban of both chemical warfare and biological warfare weapons would be extremely difficult to achieve.

As President Nixon stated, biological warfare "has massive, unpredictable, and potentially uncontrollable consequences. It may produce global epidemics and profoundly affect the health of future generations." Although we have decided unilaterally to dispose of our biological warfare stockpiles and to restrict our biological research to techniques of immunization and measures for controlling the spread of disease, we believe the security of all countries would be enhanced by a widely accepted treaty commitment that would reduce the risk that the deliberate spread of disease would ever be inflicted on mankind as a means of warfare.

Mr. Chairman, we believe the arms control negotiations should strive for realistic objectives and that often the most promising approach is through consideration of the separable parts of particular problems. The recent history of arms control and disarmament negotiations demonstrates very clearly that this approach can lead to important achievements.

I hope that other members of this committee will approach this issue with open minds and will not dismiss an opportunity to make concrete progress, through a practical step, by taking the position that the entire range of problems in these fields must be solved together and at the same time. I should like, however, to emphasize that in its approach to the question of chemical and biological warfare, the United States is prepared to give serious attention to all proposals which are now or which may be placed before the CCD. We are also prepared to engage in serious negotiations on any measure offering a reasonable opening for progress. But at this session of the CCD, we believe that the best hope of progress lies in negotiation of a convention banning the use, production, and possession of biological methods of warfare along the lines of the United Kingdom draft convention of August 26, 1969.

APPENDIX III

REVISED DRAFT
CONVENTION FOR THE PROHIBITION
OF BIOLOGICAL METHODS OF WARFARE
CONFERENCE OF THE COMMITTEE ON DISARMAMENT
GENEVA, AUGUST 18, 1970

THE STATES CONCLUDING THIS CONVENTION, hereinafter referred to as the "Parties to the Convention".

RECALLING that many States have become Parties to the Protocol for the Prohibition of the Use in War of Asphyxiating, Poisonous or other Gases, and of Bacteriological Methods of Warfare, signed at Geneva on 17 June 1925,

RECOGNIZING the contribution that the said Protocol has already made, and continues to make, to mitigating the horrors of war,

RECALLING FURTHER United Nations General Assembly Resolutions 2162 B (XXI) of 5 December 1966, and 2454 A (XXIII) of 20 December 1968, which called for strict observance by all States of the principles and objectives of the Geneva Protocol and invited all States to accede to it,

BELIEVING that chemical and biological discoveries should be used only for the betterment of human life,

RECOGNIZING nevertheless that the development of scientific knowledge throughout the world will increase the risk of eventual use of biological methods of warfare,

CONVINCED that such use would be repugnant to the conscience of mankind and that no effort should be spared to minimize this risk,

DESIRING therefore to reinforce the Geneva Protocol by the conclusion of a Convention making special provision in this field,

*The original documents, to which this document is a revision 2, appeared under the symbols ENDC/255 on 10 July 1969 and ENDC/255/Rev. 1 on 26 August 1969. [Footnote in original.]

DECLARING their belief that, in particular, provision should be made for the prohibition of recourse to biological methods of warfare in any circumstances.

HAVE AGREED as follows:

ARTICLE I

Each of the Parties to the Convention undertakes, insofar as it may not already be committed in that respect under Treaties or other instruments in force prohibiting the use of chemical and biological methods of warfare, never in any circumstances, by making use for hostile purposes of microbial or other biological agents or toxins causing death, damage or disease to man, other animals, or crops, to engage in biological methods of warfare.

ARTICLE II

Each of the Parties to the Convention undertakes:

    (a)   not to produce or otherwise acquire, or assist in or permit the production or acquisition of;

        (i)   microbial or other biological agents or toxins of types and in quantities that have no justification for prophylactic or other peaceful purposes;

        (ii)   ancillary equipment or vectors the purpose of which is to facilitate the use of such agents or toxins for hostile purposes;

    (b)   not to conduct, assist or permit research aimed at production of the kind prohibited in sub-paragraph (a) of this Article; and

    (c)   to destroy, or divert to peaceful purposes, within three months after the Convention comes into force for that Party, any stocks in its possession of such agents or toxins or ancillary equipment or vectors as have been produced or otherwise acquired for hostile purposes.

ARTICLE III

1.   Any Party to the Convention which believes that biological methods of warfare have been used against it may lodge a complaint with the Secretary-General of the United Nations, submitting all evidence at its disposal in support of the complaint, and request that the complaint be investigated and that a report on the result of the investigation be submitted to the Security Council.

2.   Any Party to the Convention which believes that another Party is in breach of any of its undertakings under Articles I and II of the Convention, but which is not entitled to lodge a complaint under Paragraph I of this Article, may lodge a complaint with the Security Council, submitting all evidence at its disposal, and request that the complaint be investigated.

3.   Each of the Parties to the Convention undertakes to co-operate fully with the Secretary-General and his authorized representatives in any investigation he may carry out, as a result of a complaint, in accordance with Security Council Resolution No. . . .

ARTICLE IV

Each of the Parties to the Convention affirms its intention to provide or support appropriate assistance, in accordance with the United Nations Charter, to any Party to the Convention, if the Security Council concludes that biological methods of warfare have been used against that Party.

ARTICLE V

Each of the Parties to the Convention undertakes to pursue negotiations in good faith on effective measures to strengthen the existing constraints on chemical methods of warfare.

ARTICLE VI

Nothing contained in the present Convention shall be construed as in any way limiting or derogating from obligations assumed by any State under the Protocol for the Prohibition of the Use in War of Asphyxiating, Poisonous or other Gases, and of Bacteriological Methods of Warfare, signed at Geneva on 17 June 1925.

ARTICLE VII

[Provisions for amendments]

ARTICLE VIII

[Provisions for Signature, Ratification, Entry into Force, etc.]

ARTICLE IX

1.   This Convention shall be of unlimited duration.
2.   Each Party shall in exercising its national sovereignty have the right to withdraw from the Convention, if it decides that extraordinary events, related to the subject matter of this Convention, have jeopardized the supreme interests of its country. It shall give notice of such withdrawal to all other Parties to the Convention and to the United Nations Security Council three months in advance. Such notice shall include a statement of the extraordinary events it regards as having jeopardized its supreme interests.

ARTICLE X

[Provisions on languages of texts, etc.]

7

Peace: Present Threats and Paths to Future Solutions

Bernt Ingvaldsen

When I received the request from the Hoover Institution on War, Revolution and Peace to address the conference on Peaceful Change, it presented me with a tempting challenge: to take my personal conception of the international situation under critical consideration and seek the possibilities for peace that may exist. Nothing is more important than to try to find the way to world peace, and I hope that what I am now going to say may be of some support to the pathseekers.

We live in a world full of dissension and dangerous conflict. Peace seems more distant than ever before. We have acute contrasts between East and West, and more latent contrasts between North and South; wars of liberation and revolutions on all continents are everyday occurrences, and over all hangs the danger of total war. The world is in a constant state of tension.

Per se, it is not a new situation. As long as human beings have lived on earth, cultures and nations have come into existence, developed, disappeared, and been replaced by others. The history of the world is to a great extent the history of wars; and the struggle for power between the nations continues today with unimpaired force.

During recent years, however, the dangers and consequences of war have become even more serious due to accelerated scientific, technical and industrial development. Mankind is facing an entirely new situation: modern weapons have an uncomfortably wide range of destruction; distance is no longer an obstacle to warfare; the danger of a surprise attack has become imminent; and weapons have been developed which within hours may wipe out Homo sapiens as a species.

The responsibility for the destiny of mankind rests primarily on the great powers, of which the decisive ones today are the United States and the Soviet Union. It is reasonable to take into account that other countries, particularly China, will soon become atomic powers. Behind the superpowers are a number of minor states, associated with them through blocs formed to create a balance of power giving the individual states as much safety as possible. However important these blocs are in the international situation, it is nevertheless the superpowers that have final control of atomic weapons.

The balance of power, or terror, is the most primitive method of trying to prevent war, and it may fail, through either technical errors or misunderstandings. And, in every case it leads to rearmament undertaken for fear one party might become stronger than the other and consequently feel tempted to attack. In order to attain peace, the differences between the great powers must be removed.

It is necessary to know the terrain before passable trails can be made through it; if one looks more closely at the differences between the great powers, and studies the background of the constant tension in the world, one finds in the front rank communism, with its attempts to undermine other societies in order to increase its own position of power. While the Western democracies since the Second World War have sought a stability and easing of tension which previously did not exist, in the communist countries the elements of tension have constantly increased and a threatening unease is spreading to other countries. The free world has entered a new and so far unknown phase in historical development: the road of understanding and reconciliation, which is the road of the future. Naturally, there are other factors and the picture is not uncomplicated enough to say that all tension has its origin in communism. However, where differences are not caused by communism directly, it often appears as a complicating factor.

Communism, as a concept, is the designation of a social order which rests on the idea of community in production, distribution, and consumption. Such a social order existed in some primitive tribal societies but disappeared with the evolution of tribal and family society into newer forms. As a dream, however, a dream of a measure against social inequality, communism did not disappear. It cropped up among Greek philosophers, later among the first Christians, and in the Middle Ages some religious sects tried to practice it. But there is a remarkably long leap, not merely in time, between the first Christians and the leaders of today in the Soviet Union. On the way the gospel has been converted into a caricature. One messianic element has survived in Soviet Communism: if the exhortation of Karl Marx and Friedrich Engels in the *Communist Manifesto*, "Proletarians in all countries, unite," is not followed voluntarily, the Soviet Union is willing to "save" the world by uniting them in another way. This ideological missionary movement is a cardinal point of the state of tension we are living through now, for in virtue of it the communists can permit themselves anything at all which serves their interests. The ideology legalizes and gives them a "right" to everything, even the most hair-raising injustice. The end justifies the means to such a total degree that ethical considerations are omitted as irrelevant. "Right" is what they themselves decide and what they at any time think it proper to undertake.

Paradoxically enough, this ideological missionary movement, elevated over ethical considerations, was founded on a social ethic: a regard for the liberty and welfare of the masses. The aim of the *Communist Manifesto* was the emancipation and prosperity of the masses. Today, however, more than fifty years after the communists came into power, there is every reason to ask: where are the people free and in which countries have they obtained prosperity? The answer is that these idealistic intentions have been accomplished in the West, not in the communist countries.

Is communism, then, something quite different from what it pretends to be? Communism had its genesis in the social conditions of the first industrial revolution in Western Europe, where the currents of liberty had carried the countries away from autocracy over to democracy, and where mighty conflicts had firmly established the right and importance of the individual in the minds of the people. The technical revolution extended the process of liberation. The liberation of individuals, not the least in North America, made possible industrialization which led to the abolition of poverty and the foundation of the welfare state. The development took place symptomatically under a liberal system, which later developed into a private capitalist system; this again is constantly changing.

Today, the West is on the road away from original capitalism, gradually approaching a system which lays ever larger stress on the social liability of society and which may suitably be called democratic capitalism. We in the West surely will never voluntarily abandon the driving force which has given us progress and prosperity: the liberty of the individual. It was this liberty which made it possible to combat poverty and abolish the proletariat as a class. It is this liberty which has given us the spiritual and material values we possess. It is this liberty which is the source of renewal. It is this liberty which initiates the creative part of ourselves and furnishes the breadth of spirit we need to be in accordance with our nature. It is this liberty which must, time and again, be protected and gained and utilized for renewed spiritual and material progress. It is this liberty for which communism has no room.

During the last century, when inequities in the liberal and capitalist system had not yet been corrected, and when increased wealth in the beginning caused increased social disparity, there existed favorable conditions for belief in Karl Marx's theory of catastrophe. According to his theory, the condition of the workers in the capitalist countries would gradually become worse and worse, with the result that they would have no other recourse than to engage in a class struggle, overthrow society, and establish the dictatorship of the proletariat. In its origin, therefore, communism was a social reaction to the obliquities of capitalism. From the very beginning, the object was to combat the capitalist system, carry out world revoltuion, and with all available means introduce communism everywhere. Through this clearly aggressive goal, communism contained a built-in threat of war; countries with a different concept of society were automatically enemies of communism and exposed to menace from it. The revolutionary thesis of Marx, however, never gained much support among the people of the world. Workers and farmers, and the large majority of people in the lower income groups usually adhered to the reform policies of the democratic parties.

No nation has voluntarily chosen to change to communism. The communist regimes in the world have been established through internal political coups supported by external instruments of power. Even the Russian Revolution did not start as a communist revolution for the dictatorship of the proletariat. On the contrary, it started as a revolt of the people against the dictatorship of the tsar. However, the Bolsheviks captured the revolution from the people, and the dictatorship merely got a new name. The aim of this great power was to make revolution in all countries; consequently the world has been divided into two camps, threatening the peace of the world.

Ever since the establishment of the Soviet state the communist regime has sought to expand its sphere of power over other countries and peoples. Wherever national and international antagonism exists, it has been aggravated by the attempts of communism to exploit the situation. Radical, discontented elements in the Western democracies are influenced by the Soviet Union to put forward demands and requests which the Soviet Union itself, within its own borders, does not want and has no intention of meeting. Requests are forwarded through demonstrations and strikes, which in the communist countries are totally forbidden. The Christian claim of mercy, which in spite of all human errors and shortcomings nevertheless is respected and followed by the West, is exploited in order to impair the West both materially and psychologically. Even Christian ideas are utilized by communism to undermine confidence in the order and form of our society. In many places extensive communist infiltration and underground work is going on, plus extensive military and technical espionage. Since the Second World War, the Soviet Union has poured billions of rubles into a global network of infiltration and espionage, to the injury of everybody's wish for peace and tolerance in the world.

The actual situation in international politics shows that simultaneously with the Western Powers having bestowed liberty on their earlier colonies, withdrawn from them, and consequently limited and not extended their own sphere of power, the communists have incessantly and inexorably pushed their sphere of power further and further. This development has extended so far that now it is obvious to everybody that the Soviet Union in conducting such a policy is jeopardizing world peace.

Such is the position. And confronted with this situation, we are forced to ask ourselves: what can we do to prevent the impending collapse of human society on earth?

No matter how important military preparedness and alertness may be considered, it is clear today that the sword is not the right weapon for lasting peace. The time has come to let it remain in the sheath as an antiquated means of solving international questions, and to build harmonious relations between the various countries. It has finally been realized that international peace must be built on international understanding. Fundamentally this should be simple enough, but in reality it enjoins humanity with a formidable task, for the different conditions of life on earth mean that all nations involuntarily appraise a situation from their own assumptions, and therefore in quite different ways. Because the fate of mankind is at stake, it is impossible to reject the task as infeasible, and consequently we have to attempt to understand one another as far as the limits of our intellect and empathy allow.

We have seen how we in the Western democracies regard communism. It is evident that the situation is considered differently in the communist countries, and particularly so in the Soviet Union. Through their entire history, the Russian people have lived under absolute power, under the Mongols as well as after Ivan the Terrible in 1547 let himself be crowned tsar. The liberty movements, which in other parts of Europe led the nations from absolute power to democratic government during the eighteenth and nineteenth centuries, did not manage to assert themselves in Russia. The tsar banished all progress, including the industrial revolution, from Russian soil. In 1917 the oppressed and backward Russian society—a people who did not know individual liberty because they had never experienced it—became the homeland of communism. The communist leaders of the country themselves did not know individual liberty, and they inherited not merely an isolationist and autocratic state without democratic traditions, but at the same time they inherited control over great power. Therefore it is quite natural that Russia continued to be a dictatorship. When the handful of communists seized power, the domestic political situation in the country was chaotic and the foreign policy faced the fundamental problems of a great power under very difficult and uncertain conditions. The Soviet Union was looked upon by everybody with distrust, and the Soviet leaders felt themselves menaced. The situation determined the policies of the leaders: continued use of power internally, and increasing tension on the foreign front. The situation aggravated the system, and the system aggravated the situation.

In the communist countries there exists no freedom of opinion or of information; both are determined by the leaders, based on political and tactical considerations. Because the capitalist states of the West oppose the aggression of the communists, they are presented as aggressive and as the root of all dangers and difficulties. It was considered imperialism when the United States and the West founded NATO in order to protect themselves against the aggression of communism. The communist countries look upon their blocs as a counterbalance against our military blocs. They are afraid because the West has previously acted in an aggressive manner, and the fear of Germany especially is a vital reality for them. They are frightened by the gigantic expansion of the West in industrial potential, and to them our order of society appears just as unintelligible and distant as their order of society appears to us; their apprehension, anxiety, and terror are to them just as real as our apprehension, anxiety, and terror are to us. There is no doubt that they have a clear understanding of the catastrophic consequences of an atomic war, but they feel obliged to continue arming.

Is there any way out of this mutual policy of fright? Can the antagonism be reduced? Now, life itself is beginning to come to the relief of mankind. In their industrial policies the capitalist and communist countries have gradually been forced farther and farther away from their original dogmas, and in this respect their development is becoming more congruent. In the West, unrestrained or shortsighted economic liberty is no longer tolerated or accepted. Economic dispositions must be socially and ethically justifiable, and the state reserves the right to supervise economic life. Individual liberty is such a driving force in economic development that the state's task is merely to apply the brakes and regulate the returns in accordance with social considerations.

In the Soviet Union, industrial development, or the lack of it, proves that without the driving force inherent in the liberty of the noncommunist nations economic life cannot be compelled, just by command of the state's high authority, to expand. In the Soviet Union, as in all other countries with a socialist economy, ineffectiveness leads to comparative stagnation in production. Socialism generally entails low production, confusion in the industrial apparatus, economic trouble, and shortage of materials. On the other hand countries with a free economy today have intense activity and rapidly increasing production, giving all members of the community an ever higher standard of living. If the communist countries want to promote faster development and attain material prosperity they must give the individual more independence and allow him a freer rein. There is hardly any other way. A modern industrial state cannot function well in a centrally controlled society. So far, the Soviet Union has not adjusted itself to the tremendous demands of a modern industrial community in economic, technical, and administrative effectiveness. Far from it, the leaders of Soviet industry are dangerously restrained by the lack of opportunity to freely undertake necessary changes. A totalitarian system can hardly be combined with such an adjustment at all, but the Soviet Union has undertaken certain steps at variance with its old orthodoxy.

It may be predicted, then, that as time passes East and West will approach a similar economic system; historically, this is not a surprising turn of events. Just as the basic traits of human nature are the same everywhere and industrial development has the same prerequisites, the economic pattern will tend towards the same form. Just as the theoretical preconditons of communism have already been removed, the original conditions for the conflict between East and West will also be removed by degrees.

International society consists of diverse countries and states. Each state has its distinctive character, has come into existence under certain climatic and geographic conditions, has been built up with certain traditions and a certain way of life, and has its base on a quite concrete and special historical foundation. Previous history is a vital part of the essence of a state, and its future depends first of all on its ability to preserve its historically conditioned way of life, its roots as a nation, and its intrinsic foundation. The primary requirement of a nation is the confidence that it may live its life as it wants to, with the certainty that its integrity will be respected by outsiders and that nobody will take away from it the special way of life which is an essential part of it.

Communism has succeeded in subjecting a number of other nations and in compelling them to accept a way of life contrary to their nature. The development in these countries is determined completely by the communist party, which—in spite of amounting to only a fraction of the population—represents the will of the nation, or which is by definition the will of the people. In the long run, this condition cannot last, for it is based on artificial constructions which contain the germ of the dissolution and destruction of the system. A system contrary to nature cannot be maintained, not even by employing force. Sooner or later a movement back to normal must emerge; and with its starting point in the self-preserving instinct of man this movement will not let itself be stopped before conditions are in harmony with the soul of the individual nation.

No power can do away with the need of an individual nation for self-determination. Today, this law of nature turns with particular strength against the Soviet Union, which has met with great difficulty in maintaining its hegemony over its satellites. It appears clear that the Soviet Union is not able to create a uniform system of international communism. In spite of the fact that the Soviet Union has not shunned any means to gain its end, world supremacy, and in spite of its utilization of local conflicts in furtherance of this goal, today the individual and national wish for and right to self-determination turns directly against Soviet plans. In the long run, no people will let anything be forced upon it by outsiders. Development within the communist countries is diverging ever faster along national lines. Revisionists are already partly recognized. The policies of China are increasingly directed against the Soviet Union. Just as the trees cannot grow forever into the sky, the universal ambitions of the Soviet Union will engender a counterforce which will prevent world communism from becoming a reality. In historical perspective it will undoubtedly be correct to state that the will of the people caused the shipwreck of communism.

The movement back to national self-determination and democratic conditions in the countries subjected by communism is, however, a very dangerous process for the various countries and for the peace of the world. Here our attitude toward and comprehension of the problems will be decisive, first for the prevention of armed power and war, and second for the establishment of a harmonious and peaceful community of nations. It will be wise for us in the West to remember that other peoples with their vastly different histories judge things very differently from us. The same things do not look alike everywhere. Poland, for instance, has experienced a longer period of peace since the Second World War than ever before in its history, and this fact naturally colors the background for its train of thought and its disposition.

It is not easy for us in the West to understand the position within the countries of Eastern Europe, and it is difficult for us to form an idea of the problems they will face during the transition from dictatorship to democracy. To transfer undertakings from public to private management is no simple matter. We must patiently prepare ourselves for the possibility that the transition may take time, perhaps several generations, and especially, we must abstain from condemning their slow progress toward liberty and what we call democracy. We must be elastic in our valuation of the system of government of other countries, and we must not set up too-high barriers between the various shades of democracy. If steady development is to take place without danger to peace, it must be gradual, nearly imperceptible. New possibilities must be digested gradually.

Transition from dictatorship to democracy endangers the safety of the state, and in practice such development cannot be allowed if there exists an outside menace against the country. The internal security of a country is always endangered by the struggle which may arise when a change in leadership is taking place, and any untimely interference may counteract its own purpose. The smallest step in the right direction nevertheless means a considerable gain, and our task must be to ensure that we in no way imperil the stability, through impatience with absolute demands or through a disapproving attitude; our task must be to facilitate development by seeing the situation as it looks on the spot to those particularly concerned. And not the least of our tasks must be to keep our own societies healthy and to be on guard against all moral decline; to prevent subversive results of misunderstood or asocial exercises of liberty; to promote personal feelings of responsibility toward the community; and to prevent materialism from undermining our sense of the higher and eternal values on which our civilization rests and which are the basis of our existence.

There are widely different forms of government in the various countries of the world, and it does not serve the cause of peace or the interests of any people to demand that our form of government be introduced where it does not fit or where it has no possibility of operating satisfactorily. International understanding depends on the comprehension of conditions of life in other countries, and on an awareness that just as countries and conditions can never be alike, neither can the various forms of government be alike. In the democracies we are even obliged to accept the fact that many states are not yet mature enough for democratic government, and consequently it may not now be appropriate for them. What these countries need are stable conditions and a basis for development, growth, and progress. When this cannot occur in a democratic way, some kind of control is needed, at least in a period of transition. Democracy is not only a new and insecure form of government, but also a responsible way of life which presupposes advanced spiritual and material maturity. The introduction of common democracy in Norway, for instance, took more than one hundred years, and it will be a long-range business in all countries which have still not found their way to the democratic form of government. Elasticity and realism in judgment are therefore essential.

In our struggle for peace we must provide material and technical assistance to countries and peoples that have lagged behind in development. This assistance will fail in its objective, however, and merely create chaos if it is not furnished in the same unselfish spirit and disposition which characterizes the religious missionary movement, and if it is not based on the principle that every country will be enabled to govern itself. In reality, wealth does not consist of material values, which time disintegrates. The real nature of wealth is the possession of mental creative power. To bring out this creative power must be the goal of our contribution to the underdeveloped countries, for it is the only assistance which may really be called assistance, and which unselfishly enables them to secure their own welfare, prosperity, and self-respect. For the sake of the developing countries themselves, as well as for the sake of peace, we must not allow ourselves to be derailed from this goal by a guilt complex created by communist agitation and suffering with which we have had nothing to do. Peace in the world is dependent on self-supporting, self-determining, self-respecting, or in other words, creative and satisfied nations.

The fantastic fact today is that our industrial application and utilization of scientific discoveries have created possibilities in life which previously did not exist. The struggle for existence can be tempered and the basis of existence be improved for all people, no matter where they are. The daily struggle for existence can be changed to a nobler life where inner security and material sufficiency can fill the place of aggression with human solidarity and gratitude. These possibilities are open to all who place human life higher than ideological passions and political ambitions. In reality, these possibilities form the most realistic paths to peace which have at any time been open to mankind.

In our efforts to secure peace, we must also take into account the universal fact that all nations, our own included, instinctively consider whatever is different with a certain hostility. People guard themselves, more or less consciously, against anything alien. This deeply human characteristic is one of the most dangerous enemies of peace. And on the whole, human beings today are as they have always been. They will take care of themselves, their family, and their community. They are afraid of everything which is strange and new; they cling to established facts. Their own opinions are the right ones, the truth. In some way or other, all people are still primitive inasmuch as they all possess a feeling of loyalty which is too narrow and no longer harmonizes with the world of today. A new consciousness, however, the consciousness of the common destiny and solidarity of the nations, is advancing at a rapid speed. We have become directly dependent on one another and we are beginning to realize this. The intercourse between the nations is beginning to abolish the false concept of isolationism and its dangerous consequences to peace. When we finally reach the point where our spiritual development has caught up with technical developments, and our innermost being has adapted itself to the outward conditions of the world today, we will discover that all people, including the "strangers" whom we looked upon as dangerous enemies, are the friends of peace.

Let us hope that a persistent wish for peace in the East and in the West, in the North and in the South, in thought and mind, in the hearts' quiet prayers everywhere on earth may engender a power which finally will elevate life to a higher level and transform the world from militant chaos to a human community.

8

International Law and Organization:
Their Influence for Peace

Sir Percy Claude Spender

My task is to speak of the part international law and organization may play in the quest for world peace. This is, I find, one of some difficulty. It is easy enough to argue with considerable truth that international law and organization have, in the last one hundred years or so, played a significant part in bringing a sense of order and peaceful progress into world relations. This established, the next step, also an easy one, is to project the view that this sense and this progress will increase in volume and influence leading ultimately, though gradually, to acceptance by the nations of the world of the discipline of law in the settlement of disputes between them, especially those likely to lead to a breach of the peace. If man can conquer space, what, it may be asked, is there to prevent him from so arranging the affairs of nations and their peoples that war shall be no more? To this the answer surely must be: there is nothing to prevent him from doing just this—except man himself.

Having made a case on these lines it would seem reasonable enough to conclude that since man is (so it is said) a rational being, the aim of international law must be to fashion acceptable norms of international conduct which can be translated by nations into common practice and thus transmuted into international law, to which each of them, in the conduct of their affairs, would submit. This is the road, it is said, that must be followed however arduous, however long it may prove to be.

The trouble with this thesis, however, is that man alone stands between himself and his salvation. He is not altogether a rational being. Neither international law not international organization can banish the scourge of war until human beings are able to restrain an urge to destroy one another in struggles for power or territory or prestige or glory or national objectives.

Man is not a peace-loving animal. The drums of war appear to possess a fatal attraction for him, especially when mass instincts are aroused, as they may so easily be by skillful and unscrupulous propaganda.

Twice in this century, in two world wars, millions of people have done their utmost to slaughter one another. Twice the cities where men, women, and children dwell have in vast measure been laid in ruins. Twice the harvest fields of warring nations have been dunged with rotten death. Twice the nations, in expiation of a sense of guilt after victory, have sought to elevate high moral concepts into norms of international behavior—first in the Covenant of the League of Nations, later in the Charter of the United Nations. Twice in our century international organizations, designed to place reason over armed might, have been established by nations victorious in war, believing or affecting to believe, in the euphoria which not unnaturally comes when the guns suddenly become silent, that war would at last be outlawed. Twice we have found that the central foundations upon which each of these organizations were erected were not firm. War, or the danger of war, appears to be mankind's constant companion.

Man and the rat, it has been said, are the only animals who are prone to kill their own kind. One would wish to believe that in the human race at least, this trait would have been, by sad experience through the centuries, obliterated. Yet the many millions of men, women, and children who in the past fifty to sixty years have in war, or in cold blood, been destroyed by fellow humans, gives us scant reason to think this urge to kill will soon disappear. Oddly enough, the greatest deterrent to global conflict in this nuclear age is perhaps man's massive capacity to destroy his fellow creatures. Great fear may prevail where reason has failed.

It is then a bloody background against which we in this decade talk of world peace. Yet no man must despair. Much can be done by international law and international organization to take us, little by little, along the path to a peaceful world. We would, however, be unwise to ignore or minimize the obstacles that lie in our way. To underestimate the magnitude of our task is to fail to understand it.

There are, as we know, a multitude of international organizations, the great majority of which are unable, except occasionally and in an indirect way, to further the cause of peace. It will not be of them that I will speak, however important in creating friendly relations and understanding between nations some of these are. I am concerned, rather, with organizations established to keep the peace.

The contribution of international organizations to the cause of peace may conveniently be examined by taking as our starting point the Hague Convention and Declaration of 1899. The nineteenth century witnessed an increasing recognition of arbitration as an appropriate means for the settlement of disputes between states. International arbitration has its roots deep in antiquity. Its growth in the nineteenth century, however, and its progress owed much to the Jay Treaty of 1794 between the United States and Great Britain and the three mixed commissions which were set up to settle certain important questions between these two countries. The concept continued to attract attention in the civilized world and the Alabama Claims Arbitration in 1872 between the same two nations led to arbitral tribunals functioning with marked success in almost a hundred cases before the close of the century. There can be no doubt that this satisfactory development for peaceful settlement of disputes owed much to the efforts and writings of international jurists.

When the Hague Conference of 1899 convened, the climate seemed favorable to the acceptance of arbitration as providing suitable machinery to resolve disputes between states; a civilized substitute for force. And one of the fruits of its labors was the Convention on Pacific Settlement of International Disputes, and the establishment of what was called, or miscalled, the Permanent Court of Arbitration.

This body still exists though its services are rarely utilized. Whenever it does function it is on an almost wholly consensual basis. States must not only be willing to submit the dispute between them to arbitration, they must also agree on the questions to be submitted and the arbitrators to be appointed. Though called a court, it has no corporate character. It is rather a panel of about 150 to 200 persons from whom arbitrators may be selected. The services of this "court" were availed of in different international disputes in a number of instances until just before the outbreak of the First World War. Only on rare occasions since has it functioned. From 1931 on, recourse to it has been made on but four or five occasions.

The Convention which led to the creation of this court did recognize that disputes between states normally ought to be settled peaceably by third-party arbitrament, which appeared to be definite progress. It is, however, by no means certain that the states which agreed to this Convention really intended to make it work. These were the days of the emperors and the kings with their armies and navies, their pomp and ceremony, and their vast powers over their peoples. One is inclined to think that the concept of peaceful settlement of disputes between states, largely the result of the writings of continental jurists, had little impact upon these rulers of the nations of the world. Even today, when all but a few of the emperors and kings have departed from the stage, many of the present leaders of nations, though proclaiming their belief in an international rule of law, pay it little more than lip service.

The first attempt on an international plane to establish machinery for the settlement of disputes, to substitute justice for aggression or the threat of aggression, must be considered to have failed. Perhaps it was doomed to fail since the nations who gathered at the Hague in 1899 assumed in their discussions that future wars were inevitable. There seems little doubt that cynicism on the outcome of the Conference was the companion of more than one of the representatives who gathered at the Hague in 1899. Their thoughts were less of peace than they were of war, or the use of force when this was considered feasible or expedient.

The comparative calm of the first decade of the twentieth century was broken when in 1914 the world was plunged into war. I was then a youth of sixteen years, and I can recall, in my own country, the enthusiasm with which men volunteered or were persuaded to volunteer for the adventure of overseas service, little aware of the human tragedy and destruction that lay ahead. It was a war, so it was said, to save democracy; a war—strangely enough, if one took heed of the leaders of the belligerent states at war with one another, political and religious—that was supported by God. *Gott mit uns* found its echo on the other side.

When the slaughter and the carnage had ended, when the cries of the wounded and afflicted were no more to be heard, when the countless dead had been buried—alas, many of them soon forgotten—thoughtful humans sought ways to end wars and thought they had found it in the organization of the League of Nations.

It was an imperfect organization, as was its Covenant. It was inescapable, perhaps, that this should have been so. Each represented a compromise between different schools of thought. All those who fashioned it did not share the ideals of Lord Cecil of England, or of Woodrow Wilson of the United States. Yet, however imperfect the organization set up, it did represent a very important step forward in man's search for universal peace.

But the political leaders were not prepared to forsake war, to submit in any real sense to the discipline of third-party arbitrament in the settlement of disputes between their countries and others. The nations, parties to the Covenant, did agree that a dispute between them likely to lead to a rupture should be submitted by them to arbitration, or to judicial settlement, or to an inquiry by the Council of the League. They did not, however, bind themselves to abide by the result. But they did agree not to resort to war for a period of three months after the award of the arbitrator, or the judicial decision, or the report of the Council. This at least was something. Any process which halts the outbreak of hostilities and provides time for reflection, mediation, or conciliation and diplomacy is important in the preservation of peace.

The draftsmen of the Covenant, unable to do more than the political leaders permitted them, did, however, include in the Covenant a provision that if the Council of the League—excluding the states parties to the dispute—was unanimous in its report, the states members of the League would be obliged not to go to war with a state party to the dispute, which complied with the Council's recommendations. A similar position resulted where a dispute had been dealt with by an arbitral award or judicial decision. If any member state should resort to war in disregard of any of these covenanted obligations, it would be deemed an act of war against all members of the League. It then became the duty of the Council to recommend to the governments concerned what effective military, naval, or air units the member states should contribute to forces designed to protect the League's covenants.

The terms of the Covenant were imperfect, cumbersome, and crude. The powers of the Council, subject in their exercise to the role of unanimity, were gravely restricted. Yet the machinery of the League could have functioned with reasonable effectiveness; much could have been done to achieve the purpose the League was designed to serve had all the states who became members, or an important and influential majority of them, been prepared to observe not merely the words of the Covenant but the spirit which breathed upon it and gave it existence, expressing, as it did, the deep desire of vast millions of people that war should be no more.

Born in an atmosphere of great hope, the League, though in its first years it went about its work with commendable enthusiasm, did not survive for long. The separate interests of the more powerful nations, the ambitions of certain political leaders, the lack of resolution of others, and the apathy of peoples, combined together to drive it to its destruction. Within the short space of two decades it fell into ruins in the disaster of another and more terrible world war. All that remains of it is history.

For some centuries before 1920 philosophers had given much thought to the problem of how nations acting together might banish war. Kant in his *Zum ewigen Frieden* (1795) was one of the great protagonists. Conceptual ideas really found their first organic expression in the League of Nations. It failed. Political and economic machinery alone proved unequal to the task. It is for consideration whether there are not certain deep psychological factors that predispose peoples to war, especially when they are under the influence of unscrupulous leaders.

As if mankind had at last learned its lesson, however, we turned from war in 1945 to create another kind of world—and another international organization— this time called the United Nations. Those who have been united in war would now, so it was said, unite for permanent peace.

How has the United Nations fared as an instrument for peace? It is difficult to be quite objective in answering this question. Either one believes, as I do, in the United Nations, since despite obvious weaknesses in its structure and functioning it represents the best that man has yet been able to devise to achieve permanent peace and save us from another blood bath, or one has lost faith in it and cares little about it. Yet in order that justice and no less than justice is done in answering this question, one must neither exaggerate its achievements in the cause of peacekeeping nor deliberately overlook its shortcomings.

Is there reason to fear that the pattern, and fate, of the United Nations will in the end follow that of its predecessor? The Charter of the United Nations is a much stronger and wider document than the Covenant of the League. Not only does it recognize, which the Covenant failed to do, that the maintenance of international peace involves the betterment of the lot of man, respect for human rights, and the termination of colonial exploitation; it establishes a specific organ—the Security Council—invested with special powers whose function it is to determine the existence of any threat to the peace of the world, and obliges it to make recommendations or to decide what measures should be taken under the Charter to maintain or restore international peace and security. The measures may be military, economic, or diplomatic. In order to enable the United Nations to take urgent military measures, member states are bound to hold "immediately available" national air force contingents for combined international enforcement action—an obligation that seems to have been conveniently forgotten by the majority of member states; and on the call of the Security Council, and in accordance with agreements to be negotiated "as soon as possible," to make armed forces available to it—another obligation which soon died on the vine.

Elaborate provisions are contained for the establishment and functioning of a Military Staff Committee consisting of no less personages than the chiefs of staff of the five permanent members of the Council. Conveniently, as it transpires, "representatives" of the chiefs of staff could function in their stead, and mercifully, I would think, all questions relating to the command of all forces at the disposal of the Council were left to be worked out, if they ever will be, subsequently.

Although all these provisions give an appearance of strength, in practice they have amounted to very little when judged against the functions and duties the Council, the Military Staff Committee (which has had but a shadowy and unreal existence), and member states were intended to perform.

In Article 2 of the United Nations Charter is contained the obligation of all member states to refrain in their international relations from the threat or use of force against the territorial integrity or political independence of any state, or in a manner inconsistent with the purposes of the United Nations—an obligation which has sadly enough been broken, and with impunity, by more than one state.

The United Nations is better organized and better equipped than the old League. It functions under a stronger charter. But we have learned that the language in which such a document is cast matters not if the states bound by it do not, in good faith, live up to its purposes or fail to act in accordance with its terms and its spirit.

Despite the existence of the United Nations it is open to doubt whether the world is safer today than it was in 1945. Whatever sense of comparative security humans may feel today is probably as much, if not more, due to the massive and awful might of two nations and the thralldom in which we are held by the nuclear bomb, as to the United Nations. The uncertain peace the world enjoys is determined by man's capacity to destroy others, rather than by any intense desire of nations to dwell in amity one with another, accepting a common international ethic.

Why is it that many organizations and intergovernmental agencies established by or under the aegis of the United Nations concerned with what may be called the nonsecurity fields, such as the World Health Organization, the Food and Agriculture Organization, the World Meteorological Organization, UNESCO, and many others, have done such remarkable and constructive work while the Security Council and the General Assembly have not sufficiently lived up to the expectations of those whose hopes have been reposed in them?

The Charter was based on the assumption that the five great powers would unite to preserve the peace, which at great sacrifice had been won principally by their efforts. The crudity of power politics was to be displaced by reason. On this assumption the Security Council was created. The veto accorded each of the great powers with permanent seats on the Council was seen by many as a counterpart of an expected unity, as an instrument not of frustration but to aid wise deliberation and produce agreed action. It was considered by most nations as the necessary price to be paid for a unity which it was assumed the great powers would bring to the discharge of their high duty.

It was not long before this assumption was proved false. Power politics were and have remained very much alive indeed. The separate national interests of permanent members of the Council soon, and too frequently, dominated the stage. It may fairly be said that when any permanent member uses its veto it is hardly likely to be done in the supreme interests of the United Nations, in the interests of all people throughout the world.

There can be little doubt that, in practice, the veto has shackled the labors and usefulness of the Council. It is however not the mere existence of the veto which can explain its shortcomings in performance. The fault lies in its use: how it is used and the reasons for its use. Too frequently it is used not in the cause of international peace, but in the advancement or protection of the separate political and power interests of this or that permanent member.

The General Assembly is not plagued by a veto. Its activities are not influenced so much by power politics as by individual and purely national interests or nationalistic ambitions. In a way this is not surprising since the General Assembly, somewhat inaccurately but frequently referred to as a "Parliament of Nations," is a body where conflicting state interests necessarily and naturally must find expression. It should, however, be firmly stated that the General Assembly is not a place in which to peddle the narrow, even selfish, nationalistic interests or aims of any nation or group of nations. The General Assembly should be concerned principally with issues and matters vastly more important, in the consideration of which the individual interests of states should be subordinated to the high international purposes set forth in the Charter of the United Nations. This is especially so when the General Assembly is discussing questions concerned with the maintenance, preservation, or restoration of peace.

Yet unfortunately, this cannot be said to be standard practice within the Assembly. It would be a misapprehension to think of the General Assembly as a truly deliberative body exclusively directing its energies, within its competence under the Charter, to the achievement of the objectives of the United Nations. Too often the Assembly is used for purely national, not international, purposes. It is hardly to be wondered at that the Assembly is being submerged under a torrent of words, words, and more words, so often the outpouring of sectional, national, and individual interests and vanities.

There is, moreover, an increasing disposition within it to disregard the terms of the Charter and to assert lawmaking or quasi-lawmaking powers. There are many good people who believe in a world parliament. The Assembly is, of course, nothing of the sort. Its authority is found in, and only in, the text of the Charter. It has no power to make laws binding on members of the United Nations. Its power is principally and almost wholly to make recommendations on a wide spectrum of matters, recommendations which member states are not obliged to accept. Nor has it power, directly or indirectly, to compel any state to accept its recommendations.

The moral force of recommendations made by the Assembly, particularly those within the field of international peace and security, can be very great, the more so when they reflect the wise deliberation of that body. They may, for example, activate the creation of international norms of conduct through the acceptance and putting into practice of recommendations made by it. This moral force will tend to be dissipated, even destroyed, if the Assembly, in disregard of the Charter, asserts powers it does not possess.

There are certain groups of states in the General Assembly which more than just occasionally have used their numbers to secure the passage of resolutions in pursuit of their own group or nationalistic ends, or as political weapons against other states to which they are opposed or antagonistic.

The Assembly has great power to fashion world opinion, which in turn may influence the conduct of nations. Though its membership has doubled since the United Nations was established less than twenty-five years ago, it cannot be said that its influence in the cause of world peace has increased; if anything, it has diminished.

The United Nations nonetheless had for the first ten years or so of its existence a creditable record of peacekeeping. In 1946 it played a notable part in the withdrawal of Soviet troops from Iran, and of British and French troops from Syria and Lebanon. In 1948 and 1949 it contributed to the cause of peace, first in bringing about a cease-fire between Pakistan and India in their dispute over Kashmir, and later in keeping the fighting between the Arab states and Israel under some control. In 1950 and 1951 there was its defense of South Korea against aggression from the north, though this was due largely to the adventitious though deliberate absence at the crucial time of the Soviet Union from the Security Council.

Then in 1956 there was the decisive intervention, this time through the actions of the General Assembly, in the Suez Canal trouble. On this occasion the General Assembly was able to act with such success because of the Uniting for Peace Resolution, carried by the General Assembly in 1950, in virtue of which, failing action by the Security Council, it asserted the right itself to act to preserve or restore peace. Whether this Resolution will be of much avail in the future to deal with situations threatening the peace is questionable, not just because its validity may be open to challenge but because of the attitude of two permanent members of the Security Council in refusing to pay their share of the expenses incurred in peacekeeping operations in Egypt and the Congo on the ground that under the Charter, the Security Council alone is competent to take action to prevent a breach of, or maintain, or restore peace, and that these expenses were not incurred under its authority.

The sad fact is that 1956, the year that witnessed the swift and successful intervention of the United Nations in the Suez trouble, witnessed also the ignominious impotence of that organization in the face of brute force on the part of a major power unresponsive to its resolution. Soviet Russia in deliberate breach of the Charter, invaded Hungary—as twelve years later it did Czechoslovakia—and contemptuously disregarded a request by the General Assembly to withdraw. Experience to date would suggest that the United Nations will remain impotent in the face of defiance by a powerful state no matter what breach of international law she may commit; except, perhaps, in the unlikely event that the state in question is not a permanent member of the Security Council and all the permanent members thereof are in agreement on action to be taken.

There is no use shutting one's eyes to the fact that during the last ten years or so the record of the United Nations in preserving the peace and restraining aggression has not been very impressive. Still it remains the hope of mankind—there is no present substitute for it. Destroyed, we would have to rebuild it, and probably on the same foundations. Whether mankind's hopes for the United Nations will be justified will depend not so much upon the words in which the Charter is expressed, as it will upon the conduct of the member states, all of whom are solemnly bound to refrain from aggression and to respect the territorial integrity of all other states. No treaty—and the Charter is the most solemn of all treaties—is any stronger than the will of the parties to it. If they, acting in good faith one to another, are determined to carry out their obligations, the aims and purposes of the treaty are likely to be achieved. If, on the contrary, parties to a treaty seek to avoid or evade their obligations or refuse to perform them, the treaty may be completely undermined and finally collapse.

In its role as peacekeeper of the world, the United Nations is going through a critical period not altogether dissimilar to that which the League of Nations encountered in the middle thirties. Whether it proves able to live up to the prayers and expectations of millions of people throughout the world will depend upon the extent to which members of the United Nations dedicate themselves to the noble aspirations of its founders and prove willing to subordinate their individual, separate political interests and national ambitions to the common welfare and safety of men and women everywhere. We have a long way to go before this will happen.

I have, thus far, spoken of the principal political organs of the United Nations. Let us turn our attention now to its judicial organ, the International Court of Justice, of which for nine years I was privileged to be a member. The functions and jurisdiction of the Court, and the law it is bound to apply in deciding cases brought before it, are provided for in a special international statute which is part of the United Nations Charter.

The overriding purpose of the United Nations is to maintain international peace and security, and to that end to bring about by peaceful means and in conformity with the principles of justice and international law the adjustment or settlement of international disputes or situations which might lead to a breach of the peace. It was to provide a means to effectuate this purpose that the World Court, one of the three principal organs of the United Nations, was created. The Court's statute provided that its jurisdiction comprises all cases which states refer to it, and all matters specially provided for in the statute or in treaties or conventions already in force.

A wide jurisdiction has accordingly been conferred upon the Court. There is scarcely any dispute between states which could not be either resolved or assisted to resolution by the Court, if—and here is the difficult point—only states were prepared to submit their disputes to it. Submission to the Court's jurisdiction is, however, not compulsory. Attempts made in San Francisco in 1945, when its statute was being drafted, to make it so failed, and similar attempts today or in the foreseeable future would, I am convinced, meet the same fate. A majority of states through their political leaders were not then, and are not now, prepared to accept the discipline of international law to settle disputes between themselves and other states. It is not then altogether surprising, though regrettable, that of 125 members of the United Nations, less than half have agreed to submit to the jurisdiction of the Court, and of these more than a few have only agreed to do so subject to restrictive conditions.

Excuses are not lacking to explain why states who proclaim their adherence to, or give lip service to, international law are not prepared to put into practice what they profess. The law applied by the Court, it is said by some, is that of the Western world, representing Western values and not attuned to the needs of the world of today with new emerging nations possessing separate indigenous cultures. The Court, others assert, does not decide cases in accordance with what is called at large "justice," but by applying legal rules which, so it is said, stand in the way of "justice." Sometimes the contention is that the Court's procedure is cumbersome and outmoded. At times the argument is that regional courts should be established to deal with cases with dispatch, the World Court being available only as a final court of appeal. These are but some of the excuses advanced.

The real reasons why only a limited number of states are prepared to submit to the jurisdiction of the Court are to be found, not in the structures or composition of the Court or in the law it applies or in its procedure; they are to be found in the field of national politics. Political leaders of too many states are just not prepared to submit to the rule of law, and to surrender or subordinate a portion of their power or ambitions.

The truth is that neither the International Court of Justice nor any other court or system of courts which could be created in its place will be given the opportunity to discharge fully the function of international law in the settlement of disputes between states, or in dealing with situations which may lead to a breach of the peace, until political leaders are prepared to abandon force and international pressures and manoeuvers to attain their political and national ends, and are prepared to accept rules of international law and submit to its discipline. The time when they are prepared to do this is not even on the horizon. The political leaders of too many states know that only too often they can get far greater individual advantages in pursuit of their ends by political manoeuvers, pressures, threats, and the like than they are likely to receive at the hands of an objective and impartial tribunal.

The Court also has an advisory jurisdiction. It is available to certain international bodies, especially the General Assembly. On a number of occasions the Assembly has availed itself of this jurisdiction. Experience would suggest, however, that where subjective political considerations or overtones intrude greatly into an issue of any importance the Court is not likely to be asked for its objective advice, unless it is thought more than probable that it will support the views of a majority in the Assembly.

The fact is that the Security Council and the General Assembly are prevented from functioning to maximum capacity as peacekeepers by influences which are largely political and nationalistic in character. Why is this so? I wish one could be sure. An answer might be advanced with greater confidence if only we could with any certainty determine the causes of wars. We are accustomed to being told that these are usually economic or territorial in character. This is however too superficial a view. For my part I think they lie much deeper. They are to be found in man's almost automatic, involuntary response to unconscious primitive instincts which lie deep beneath the surface of civilization; instincts of cupidity, acquisitiveness, aggressiveness, assertiveness, pugnacity, self-preservation, hostility, even vanity.

These primitive characteristics are part of man's unconscious self which determine his conduct and his reactions to events and circumstances in times of national or emotional stress, perhaps more than the mores that a civilized society has been able to impose upon him.

The unconscious in the individual, determining so greatly his conduct toward his fellow men, is but the microcosm of the unconscious of the community in which he lives, of the nation or the state to which he belongs. Man in times of stress or emergency is inclined to respond more powerfully to the promptings, urgings, and influences of the unconscious—the irrational—than to the conscious or the rational. He is more likely to be propelled in the direction desired by political adventureres, by primitive stirrings, than by any appeal to reason. In short, the causes of war are closely associated with psychological factors operating within the unconscious mental functioning of men and women. Primitive instincts, such as those of self-preservation, in the face of real or imagined danger, are apt to beget fear. Fear begets aggression and so on and so on.

History can provide many examples of political leaders who have been aware of the unconscious urge of otherwise rational people to aggressive conduct once primitive instincts slumbering in the unconscious are aroused. Great demagogues appear to have a peculiar capacity to arouse the unexpressed fears and longing of the people they lead or mislead. Hitler provides a striking example. He was able to inflame and stimulate the German people to war not just because of his strident, mesmeric, demoniac oratory, but because he was able to excite the unconscious urgings of the mass of the people for prestige, for revenge, for victory, for gain, for power over others.

States of today with their complexity, their constant emphasis on nationalism, their increasing governmental controls, their power over the lives and thinking of citizens, and their dominion or influence over the media of education and communication present an ever-increasing challenge to the preservation of human liberties and to world peace, because of the opportunity afforded political opportunists to condition the people's responses and actions.

The kings no longer dwell in the Halls of Power. Other leaders have taken their places. Some have achieved leadership by armed force, or by deceit or corruption. Others have done it by democratic, or so-called democratic, processes. Still others have used democratic machinery to elevate themselves to despotic power. However, or by whatever means, the rulers of today have come to authority over their people, they are not likely to surrender authority willingly. More likely they will cling to power by such means as are open to them. One of these, the most potent of all, is nationalism, with its evocative appeal to the blind, primitive instincts of mean and women. Nationalism provides a ready tool in the hands of the seekers of power.

The organized savagery and devastation of modern warfare find their origin in the wars of religion of the sixteenth and seventeenth centuries. The cruel ferocity of these wars after some decades of comparative quiet was followed in the latter part of the eighteenth and early in the nineteenth century by wars of nationalism, which in recent times have progressively become more terrible in their savagery.

The growth and final victory of religious tolerance over intolerance brought the wars of religion to an end and the nations, for a while, enjoyed calm and moderation. Only too soon, however, another and more powerful intolerance arose—its name was nationalism. Like a weed it has spread to different parts of the world. It is this baleful influence which has limited so much the work of international organizations concerned with peacekeeping, and the efforts of international law to reduce areas of conflict between states and bring order into their relations.

Once nationalism stood for struggles against despotism and oppression and the like. Today it rarely does. It has become too frequently a powerful political instrument in the hands of unscrupulous, or ambitious, or chauvinistic political leaders.

Nationalism in its modern manifestation is something quite different from patriotism. A patriot is one devoted to his country and the well-being of its people. Today's nationalist is rarely a patriot, though, of course, he may be one. He is usually concerned with power or those things which go with power. Patriotism finds its natural expression in community service; nationalism tends to feed on self-interests pursued regardless of others, and its identification with so-called national interests is usually a cover for schemes to preserve or achieve political authority and as an instrument to attract and hold public support. Nationalism is rarely moderate in its demands or in the means it pursues. By its very nature it is antithetical to internationalism.

Within the United Nations we have observed nationalism and the peddling of separate national interests steadily eating away the authority of that organization as the peacekeeper of an organized world.

Nationalism is a greater force in the world than any political or economic ideology. It lifts its head in many parts of the world encouraging hostility and strife. It breeds mental attitudes conducive to conflict and adverse to international peace. There surely is little doubt that the great wars of this century have been those of nationalism. Nor can there be any doubt that wars, even of great dimensions, are possible between states whose political and economic structures are substantially similar because of nationalistic ambitions and aspirations. The present hostile relationship between Soviet Russia and Communist China provides an example of opposing nationalism taking up belligerent attitudes which not inconceivably could project armed conflict on a massive scale.

It would be a sterile performance to speak of the role of international organizations and international law, except against the backdrop of the world in which we live. It is a splendid world if mankind is prepared to live in peace and is permitted to do so. Yet the peoples of vast areas of it are not yet so prepared or permitted. Those who believe in peace under an international rule of law and who work to do all they can to bring it about must stand somewhat appalled at the immensity of the task before them.

Whatever individuals may do will not be enough. Their efforts are likely to make but a comparatively minor impact. Yet that impact can be an important one. It is the people present at these discussions who are able critically to mould public opinion in our respective countries and wherever freedom of thought and inquiry is permitted. Hopefully, in the end we may see the influence of our ideas extended to or reflected in other countries where today freedom of thought and speech is denied.

It is, however, international organizations, not individuals, that play the major part in the battle for peace. Of these organizations the most important are the Security Council and the General Assembly. Our aim should be to restore to their intended authority the high and noble purposes each was designed to serve. We must judge the performance and conduct of member states and their representatives in each of these bodies solely by the manner and extent to which they serve these purposes. We must be fearless in publicly criticizing the states, large or small, who use the United Nations not in discharge of their international obligations to it, but to push their, or their group's, special interests and ambitions, refusing to subordinate them to the international obligations which they have so solemnly undertaken. It is not enough that nations proclaim their belief in international law and their devotion to the principles which govern the United Nations. What is needed is that nations put this belief into practice.

The Western world, whose members proclaim their belief in international justice and the rule of law, has over the last ten to fifteen years, within the United Nations and outside it, stood aside and witnessed more than once, almost without protest, the clear and solemn obligations of the Charter of the United Nations being breached and disregarded as if it were something which was no concern of theirs. It has witnessed the gradual erosion of the authority of the United Nations due to the elevation of limited and selfish national interests over those of the world at large. It stands almost mesmerized by its own affluence and by the myths it has itself created, or helped to create, in its desire to preserve that affluence and to avoid any trouble or any interference with its comforts and enjoyment. Its people, and its leaders, are only too ready to believe what they want to believe.

Twenty-five years ago my friend Walter Lippmann expressed the belief that a stable and enduring peace could be established in an alliance between the United Kingdom, the Soviet Union, and the United States, provided they could agree to promote a kind of settlement in Europe and Asia that did not bring them into conflict. Many thought along similar lines. Indeed, the Security Council with its five permanent members as constituted in 1945 reflected a not dissimilar idea. All that was needed to bring this about was, so it was thought, a little wisdom and tolerance on the part of each of the nations concerned.

The stable and enduring peace which Lippmann and others hoped would come to pass has proved to be, so far, just not within reach. And despite the clear pattern of international conduct of the Soviet Union in the years from 1947 on, the Western world reveals an odd willingness to accept as true the myth that the Soviet Union's global strategy and objectives have changed fundamentally; that she has been moving gradually but constantly in the same direction as Europe and the United States; that liberty, and freedom of thought, speech, and from fear is being restored to her people; that she is undergoing a process of liberalization; that our patterns of thought and interests are bit by bit coming closer together. The wish is, of course, father to the myth. But myths provide no basis on which to conduct international relations, or to endeavor to establish an enduring peace.

No one would wish to see a return to the days of the cold war; and one would indeed wish to be as tolerant as possible of the conduct of all nations. There is, however, a vast chasm between mere tolerance and indifference. To be tolerant of the faults or conduct of others is a good thing. To be indifferent, as the Western world has been, to the Soviet Union's deliberate and premeditated breach of the United Nations Charter in its rape of Czechoslovakia—as of Hungary not so long before—does not help the United Nations or the cause of peace. Such has been this indifference that today one has become accustomed to hear Soviet propaganda in defense of its action taken up and repeated with almost implied approval by Western nations. One almost is persuaded that the Soviet Union contributed by this cruel deed to the stability of Europe and to the benefit of us all.

To be tolerant of such conduct, to be indifferent to the brutal denial of self-determination to a brave people and the imposition upon them of a Stalin-like reign of terror merely encourages the wrongdoer. I thought we had learned that in the nineteen thirties. It lessens the dignity and standing of the states that so willingly accept the situation; it fractures the norms of international conduct; and it erodes the world organization's authority, obligations to which have been cynically and deliberately ignored.

Surely this sad event called at least for full debate within the United Nations and its condemnation of Soviet conduct. But the majority of its member states were only too prepared to find an excuse or justification for doing nothing in the request not to intervene of a government acting under the intolerable and evident duress of the wrongdoer. It is hardly to be wondered that many people think that the United Nations has become an association where there is one law for the powerful and another for others.

From the agonies of the two great wars of this century we now have a breathing space within which to protect ourselves from greater disaster. Unless we are wise this disaster could well overtake us. We live in a dangerous world in which it would almost seem that there are active forces for evil at work to bring the tragedy of global conflict upon us again. Who can today view the arms race between the United States and the Soviet Union—a race now joined by Communist China—and the even more terrible weapons being devised, except with a sense of foreboding? Our hopes for peace continue to reside in the United Nations. It can succeed, however, only if member states discharge their Charter obligations without reservations and with courage, and in good faith give it unqualified support.

One thing is certain: if the United Nations should fail as a peacekeeping organization, the outlook for us all will be somber indeed.

If, in this essay, I have emphasized the obstacles which stand in the path of peace, it is because it is wiser to know what these are than pretend to believe they do not exist. Yet if we can forestall the outbreak of another large-scale war for the rest of this century, it is my hope, indeed my belief, that mankind will come to realize that world peace can be secured if nations are prepared in their international conduct to submit to the discipline of accepted rules or norms of international conduct; in other words, to accept and submit to international law. World peace through law is something more than a mere slogan.

—9—

Ideologies of Violence and Social Change

Sidney Hook

I

That wars begin in the minds of men is one of the insights that inspired the organization of UNESCO. It is a truth that makes the education of a country, the ideals of its school systems and their underlying ideology, not a purely domestic matter but a subject of international concern. It becomes not less true when we acknowledge that the minds of men are molded by the history, culture, and institutions in which they have developed. The conflicts of interest *in* any given society and *between* different societies will inescapably reflect themselves in the minds of those who live in them.

So long as men remain men, conflicts of interest will remain integral to the human condition. That is why the perspective of peace cannot be guaranteed merely be establishing agreement or unity in the minds of men independently of the social institutions in which they have been nurtured. That is why no purely internal transvaluation of values can bring peace in society or among nations unless accompanied by profound institutional change. Even a shared interest in survival without some institutional means of resolving conflicts among other interests will not guarantee peace.

One of the perennial illusions of human thought is that it can exist apart from its institutional matrix. That illusion expresses itself in myriad ways—sometimes in the belief that a common ideology is a sufficient or even necessary condition of peace. Sometimes the chief weight is placed on a common tradition or a common language on which the hopes for peace hang. Yet we know that some of the fiercest wars have been fought among those who have shared the same fundamental *Weltanschauung*, for example, in the great wars of religion. The greatest military conflict in world history up to that time was waged during the American Civil War between the North and South whose basic traditions and language were common.

On the other hand, we know that nations can and have lived in peace with different ideologies, different traditions, different languages. If world peace depended upon the establishment of a unitary world outlook, whether religious or secular, or a common language—history makes a common tradition unattainable—prospects of attaining it would be dim indeed. The existence of diversity and plurality of world outlooks, traditions, and languages is for many reasons highly desirable aside from the intrinsic value of the variety of delightful experiences it makes possible. Fortunately, it is not required to sacrifice them in order to reduce the likelihood of war between nations and within nations.

Granted, then, that the hope of peace and peaceful social change depends more upon the institutional ways of resolving differences of interest than upon common beliefs or rationalizations—in both senses of the word. Still, there are some views about the nature of man and society—some more or less systematically articulated doctrines and attitudes—which make more difficult the achievement of the institutional changes required for peace and peaceful change. The mind of man, culturally determined though it be, is not merely a passive resultant of social forces. It cannot be reduced without remainder either to the Objective Mind of Hegel or to the neural impulses of physiological psychology. It reacts selectively upon its conditions and often redetermines, in virtue of its beliefs, the direction of its own development. Thinking makes a difference, and sometimes a crucial difference, when genuine alternatives of action open up before us. To recognize the conditions out of which ideas arise is not incompatible with recognizing the great impact they may have on events. It is because of their impact that we sometimes seek to understand their origin and validity. Knowledge could never be power unless ideas made a difference. Any intelligent form of Marxism that acknowledges that men make their own history acknowledges therewith that ideas count. Otherwise what would be the point of trying to convert people to Marxism? Consciousness does not lose its importance because it has roots in social existence.

It is not only true beliefs but false beliefs, not only valid attitudes but invalid attitudes, however they be defined, that affect behavior. With respect to the prospects of peace among nations and peaceful social change within nations, it is indisputable that nationalism and racism are prejudicial to their furtherance. By "nationalism" I mean not patriotism, understood in Santayana's phrase as "natural piety for the sources of our being," but the glorification of the nation-state as privileged above others or exempt from principles of political morality in its relation to other states. By "racism" I mean not the belief that there are inherent genetic differences in capacities between ethnic groups but the belief that to the extent that there are, this justifies invidious distinctions in their social treatment, and an abandonment of the postulate of the moral equality of all persons in the democratic community. There are entire libraries devoted to the evil effects of the ideologies of nationalism and racism. It is significant that except for a handful of fanatics all representatives of these ideologies today seek to justify them defensively as nothing more than claims for compensatory inequalities to redress historic grievances.

More threatening today to world and especially domestic peace is the growth of a family of doctrines that I call the ideologies of violence. These ideologies have developed on the peripheries of movements of social protest originally fired by an idealism opposed to war and oppression. Gradually, however, they have acquired a programmatic character of their own. They assert that, to quote one writer, "The threat of violence, and the occasional outbreak of real violence (which gives the threat credibility) are essential elements in conflict resolution not only in international but also national communities."[1] Some go farther and assert that violence and the threat of violence are necessary and useful in achieving social reforms. The criticism of the use of violence is denounced as hypocritical, as a way of playing the game of the Establishment, as a reaching for a cowardly peace with it. I cannot recall any period in American history in which there has been so much extenuation and glorification of the use of violence, not as episodic forays of symbolic character to call attention to shocking evils, but as a legitimate strategy in social, political, and even educational reform. It will be recalled that John Brown, God's angry man, as well as most of those who rallied to his defense denied that his original intention was violence against persons or destruction of property, insurrection or murder but only a design to free the slaves and lead them to Canada. Up to the Civil War the leading abolitionists were pacifists.

Until recently those who defended the role of violence in social change did so in the main from a revolutionary perspective that forthrightly repudiated democracy as a political system either as a sham, covering up class rule, or as an inadequate institutional expression of self-government. The only question that faced the revolutionist when the question of violence was posed was an instrumental one—the relative cost, effectiveness, and consequences of extraparliamentary means of opposition compared with the legal means when they were available. Marxists as a rule have been opposed to *individual* acts of terror, to the propaganda of the deed as a senseless policy that plays into the hands of reaction. They recognize and endorse *class* violence. The violence of class against class is to them only an acute form of the inescapable class struggle. Daniel De Leon is the only orthodox Marxist I know who expressly declared that a constitutional victory for socialism without any violence was preferable because its legality represented a triumph for the principle of civilization. Marx himself declared that in the case of England, the United States, and Holland peaceful transition to socialism was possible. They were exceptions to the perspective of forcible overthrow. Lenin cancelled the exceptions and proclaimed the inevitability of war between the communist and noncommunist worlds in the inevitable triumph of the communist system. Lenin's disciples, especially Stalin, echoed him on this matter to the last syllable. It was Khrushchev, reluctantly convinced of the lethal possibilities of nuclear weapons, who had the courage to modify Leninist doctrine. He asserted that the victory of world communism was still inevitable but not inevitably through war. War was still possible, wars of national liberation very probable, but Armageddon was not necessary. For tactical purposes some national communist parties have cautiously put forward the non-Leninist idea that they may conquer political power without violence, especially if their opponents are accommodating enough to surrender.

I shall not pursue the analysis of the communist theory and practice of violence and its divagations from Lenin to the present because it is so frankly opportunistic in character that the real intent of communists can only be construed, not from their words, but from the constellation of forces in which they find themselves at the moment. Simple justice, however, requires the recognition that they, too, find the ideologists of violence in some countries somewhat of an embarrassment, particularly when they invoke the legacy of Lenin.

What is comparatively novel in our time is the defense of violence by those who are not prepared openly to abandon the standpoint of democracy but who, out of design or confusion, contend that a "healthy" or "just" or "progressive" democratic society will tolerate violence, recognize its productive and creative role, and eschew any strategy for the control of violence by resort to the force of the civil authorities or to police power. A report of one of the Task Forces of the National Commission on the Causes and Prevention of Violence (*The Politics of Protest*)[2] concludes by repudiating the corporational wisdom of the so-called "two-pronged approach" to violence. The first prong of this approach seeks to control or restrain the violence. The second prong attempts to meet genuine grievances by appropriate reforms and remedies. Apparently the use of "controlled force to protect civil order" while efforts are organized to cope adequately with the underlying grievances is unacceptable to the Task Force headed and directed by Professor Jerome H. Skolnick. On this view, once the demands made by those who are violent are distinguished from the causes of the violence, the major effort must go into meeting the demands, into reforming society, not into curbing violence. Society itself must accept the burden of guilt for the violence. Those who initiate the violence must be considered victims, not malefactors.

It goes almost without saying that this sympathetic approach to manifestations of violence is limited only to particular groups and to special causes. It is not generalized to hold for all public violence, especially for violence *against* good causes. It is not brought to bear on the public violence of groups enraged by the violence of the partisans of "good" causes. We are, therefore, not dealing with general principles of social action whose validity can be tested by universalizing them to assess their consistency and social consequences. We are dealing with a proposed strategy in a struggle for power—a strategy that appears both arbitrary and short-sighted not only with respect to basic principles of political justice but to important proximate goals.

There are certain common-sense objections that are flagrantly overlooked in this rejection of the "two-pronged approach." First of all, to urge that we treat primarily the *causes* of violence and not divide our energies by curbing expressions of violence, overlooks the obvious fact that we do not always know what the basic causes of violence are even when its manifestations are widespread. Second, even if we believe we know what the causes are, treating them properly, remedying the evils, changing the behavior patterns required to modify or control the situation may require time. For example, if the existence of slums is regarded as the chief cause of urban violence, something not really established in some cases, rebuilding the city ghetto or dispersing it cannot take place overnight. If violence meanwhile is not curbed, more buildings may be burned than can be constructed in the same time period. To be sure *promises* to reform the city can be easily made. And it is unfortunately true that these promises may not be kept once the danger of arson and violence is contained. But neither is it certain that violence, arson, and looting will expedite the redemption of promises of reform. To this very day the scarred remains of our riot-torn cities are gaunt and painful reminders of this. Is it not possible that the fear inspired by the violence and confrontation instead of spurring on reforms or strengthening the desire for reform may set off a counter-violence? Why is it assumed as a matter of course that violence will result in the mutual accommodation of interest rather than in further provocation and escalation of violence?

Thirdly, let us suppose we escape this danger and violence does not call into existence its own nemesis. Is there nothing illegitimate and blameworthy about the action even if it turns out successfully? Is there no socially deleterious effect of violence upon the delicate fabric of confidence and trust so essential to a civilized society, if it can be rudely torn whenever violence pays?

I shall return to these questions. I raise them here only to indicate the degree to which violation and incitement to violence are acquiring today a respectable status. They have become *salonfähig*. They are assumed to have a legitimate—in some quarters, an essential—role in the process by which consensus, even democratic consensus, is established.

In analyzing these questions I propose to state certain truths about current ideologies of violence, expose some sophistical approaches by which some ideologists of violence confuse themselves and, unhappily, others as well, and clarify the main issue obscured in most discussions.

II

One of the most frequent confusions in the apologetic literature of violence is the identification of force and violence. Since all government and law rest ultimately—although not exclusively—upon force, the universality of the actual or potential exercise of force prepares the ground for a slide to the view that violence, too, is universal and therefore an inescapable facet of all social life. Those who condemn resort to violence in a democracy are then denounced as themselves confused or hypocritical.

The differing connotations of the words "force" and "violence," the fact that in actual usage there is something strained in substituting one expression for another in all contexts, suggest that they refer to different situations or types of experience. Violence is not physical force *simpliciter* but the "illegal" or "immoral" use of physical force. That is why the term "violence" has a negative and disparaging association except when it anticipates a more acceptable state of affairs, political or moral, in behalf of which physical force is used, e. g., when "revolutionary violence" is approved.

"Force" is normatively neutral in meaning. It cannot be renounced without making ideals that encounter resistance ineffectual. Only absolute pacifists can consistently condemn the use of physical force under all circumstances. And their argument can be shown to be self-defeating or irrational, for it is apparent that the very values in behalf of which the use of force is forsworn—the preservation of life, the absence of cruelty, the avoidance of indignity—under some circumstances can be furthered only by the use of force. Force is necessary to sustain or enforce legal rights wherever they are threatened, and human rights, too, which have a moral authority of their own to justify them. Otherwise they are no more than aspirations or pious hopes. When James Meredith was denied the right to study at the University of Mississippi, when Negro women and children were prevented from attending school at Little Rock after the first school desegregation decision, it was force that protected and redeemed their rights against the violence and the threat of violence of the mob.

Whatever rules of the political game are established in order to resolve human conflicts, personal or group, force must ultimately defend or enforce the rules if they are violated. Where a party resorts to violence in order to breach those rules, to disrupt or destroy the game, it cannot justifiably *equate* its violence with the force used to sustain the rules so long as it professes allegiance to the political system defined by those rules. That is why it makes little sense to discuss the questions of force and violence in the abstract independently of the political context. What holds true for the use and limits of violence in a despotism is not true for the use and limits of violence in a democracy.

One of the most powerful justifications of democracy is that it more readily permits the resolution of human conflicts by argument, persuasion, and debate than is the case under anarchy or despotism. Under anarchy the chaos of recurrent violence defeats the possibility of consensus. Under despotism the appearance of consensus is achieved by terror, the unrestrained and unrestricted use of force. When violence breaks out in a democracy to that extent it marks the failure or the weakness of the system. Some have concluded that democracy is therefore too noble and rational an ideal to be serviceable to man. Others resign themselves to the suicide of democracy by inactivity in the face of violence. But these reactions do not exhaust the alternatives. A democracy has the moral right to protect itself. Its legitimate use of force to preserve the rules of a democratic society, to enforce the rights without which democracy cannot function, may be wise or unwise, judicious or injudicious. But such use cannot sensibly be classified as violence.

The democratic system ideally seeks to make the use of force in human affairs responsible to those who are governed, and to reduce the occasions, frequency, and intensity with which physical force is actually employed. Insofar as it expresses a moral ideal, independently of the political systems instrumental to its realization, it is that the reduction of human suffering, the elimination of pain, the avoidance of bloodshed, and the right to collective self-government are desirable.

There is much wider agreement among men on the validity of these ideals than on the best way to achieve them. Just as men can more readily agree on specific truths than on a definition or theory of truth, so they more readily agree on what is good than on theories or justifications of the good. Whatever their definition of the good is, few reflective persons will deny the proposition that "a divorce is better than a murder," or when conflict arises in social life—whether in trade unions, political organizations, or the life of nations—the proposition that "separation is better than extermination."

The importance of considering the question of violence in a *political* context is apparent when we examine some typical syndromes of apologetic justification for violence. The first was exhibited by Mr. Rap Brown, former head of SNCC, in his now classic observation in defending urban riots that "violence is as American as cherry pie." This piece of wisdom actually is the gist of the findings of several Task Forces of the National Commission on the Causes and Prevention of Violence. They gravely inform us that violence is customary in American life—as if that were news, as if that made violence more acceptable, as if the prevalence of violence proved anything more than that the democratic process in America had often broken down in the past, as if the relevant question concerned the past rather than the present and future of the democratic political process, as if the fact that something is authentically American necessarily makes it as praiseworthy as cherry pie. Certainly lynching is as American as cherry pie, but hardly a cause for boasting!

A second popular syndrome of apologetic justification for violence may be called the Boston Tea Party syndrome. Since our patriotic forbears dumped valuable property into the harbor and engaged in other acts of violence, why is it wrong, we are asked, for present-day rebels to follow suit? Here, too, it is shocking to observe both the source and the frequency of this response to criticism of violence. The SDS invoked the Boston Tea Party in their legal defense of their violence at Columbia University and elsewhere. In their case the exuberance and ignorance of youth can be pleaded in partial extenuation. But what shall we say of the adults who in a special foreword to *The Politics of Protest* wrote:

> We take the position that the growth of this country has occurred around a series of violent upheavals and that each one has thrust a nation forward. The Boston Tea Party was an attempt by a few to alter an oppressive system of taxation without representation. The validation of these men rested on their attempts to effect needed social change. If the Boston Tea Party is viewed historically as a legitimate method of producing such change, then present day militancy [i.e., violence] whether by blacks or students, can claim a similar legitimacy.[3]

This total disregard of the fact that the American colonists had no means of remedying their grievances by peaceful constitutional change is symptomatic of the grossly unhistorical approach to problems of social change. It is reinforced by the cool disregard of peaceful changes that can be won under our constitutional system by extending representation. Further, what is morally and politically permissible to a democrat struggling for freedom under despotic conditions is not permissible to him once the mechanisms of democratic consent have been established. Democracy cannot function for long if political decisions are made not by due process but by actions of street mobs, no matter how well intentioned they appear at the outset. To be sure, democratic institutions work slowly and like all institutions imperfectly. That is the price of democracy which the democrat cheerfully pays because he knows on the basis of history and psychology that the price of any other political alternative is much higher. The democrat who puts his faith in democracy knows that the majority can be wrong but he will not thereafter accept the rule of a minority because it occasionally may be right. The integrity of the process by which a minority may peacefully become or win a majority is all-important to him. If the democratic process functions in such a way as to violate the basic values of any group of citizens, they have a moral right to attempt to overthrow it by revolution, but they cannot justifiably do so in the name of democracy. And it is open to others to counter these efforts on the basis of their own revolutionary or counterrevolutionary mandate from heaven.[4]

The third syndrome challenges the contention that a principled democrat cannot reform an existing democracy by violence without abandoning his own democratic first principles. This position asserts that existing means of dissent are inadequate, that the wells of public knowledge are poisoned, that the majority has been misled by its education, corrupted by affluence, or enslaved by its passions. Allowing for certain changes in time and idiom, this indictment against democracy is as old as the Platonic critique. But Plato did not pretend to be a democrat! That the institutional life and mechanisms of American democracy are inadequate is undeniable. But just as undeniable is the fact that in many respects they are more adequate today than they have ever been in the past, that dissent has a voice, a platform, a resonance greater than ever before.

The issue is, however, this: does a democrat, dissatisfied with the workings of a democracy, strive to make them more adequate by resorting to violence? Or does he strive with all the arts of persuasion at his command to convert an unenlightened majority to an enlightened one? And what is the test of the inadequacy of existing democratic mechanisms to remedy grievances? That the minority has failed to persuade the majority? This is like saying that a democrat will be convinced that elections are truly democratic only when *he* wins them. Having failed to persuade the majority by democratic and constitutional means, the minority claims the right in the name of a hypothetical future majority to impose their opinions and rule by violence on the present majority. And by a series of semantic outrages they call this a democratic method of reforming democracy!

It is easy enough to expose this when it is—as it has often been in the past—a stratagem in the propaganda offensive of totalitarian groups. But the difficulty is greater when these contentions are put forward by individuals who sincerely believe themselves committed to democracy. What they are really saying in their sincere confusion is that in any democratic society that falls short of perfection—that is, in any democratic society in which they fall short of winning a majority—they have a democratic right to resort to violence—which is absurd. Unfortunately, as Cicero once observed, there is no absurdity to which some human beings will not resort to defend another absurdity.

The fourth syndrome in the contemporary apologetic literature of violence is the justification of the tactics of violent disruption and confrontation on the ground that the state itself employs force, and sometimes makes an unwise use of it either in war or in preserving domestic peace. Who has not heard militants of the New Left, not only students but their faculty allies, countering rebukes of their irresponsible resort to violence with the cry: "But the United States Government uses force! Therefore it cannot be wrong for us to use it." Only an anarchist who does not recognize any state authority can consistently make this kind of retort, and even anarchists would not likely be much impressed by it if it were mouthed by raiding parties of the Ku Klux Klan and similar groups. In any society, democratic or not, where the state does not have a monopoly of physical force, to which all other sanctions are ultimately subordinate, we face incipient civil war.

Nor is the situation any different when the state embarks upon actions that offend the moral sensibilities of some of its citizens. In a sharp exchange recently with a leader of radical faculty activists, I was asked: "How can you reasonably protest against the comparatively limited use of violence by the SDS at Columbia University and elsewhere [of which incidentally he did *not* approve] in view of the massive use of violence by the United States in Vietnam?" It is a retort frequently heard when student and black-militant violence is condemned. Professor Chomsky is a great admirer of A. J. Muste, the late revolutionary pacifist leader. I find it ironical that the question he asked me is the same kind of question hurled at Muste by members of the Communist Party in the thirties in rejoinder to Muste's protests against the violent disruption of the meetings of the American Workers Party of which, together with others, we were the founders. They said to Muste, "How can you bring yourself to protest against the inconsequential and largely symbolic violence of Young Communists in breaking up your meetings while Hitler is mobilizing all the violence of Fascist reaction against the European working class?" One would never have guessed from Muste's language at these junctures that he was a clergyman!

For one thing, these rhetorical questions overlook the obvious fact that one can be opposed *both* to student violence on campus and to the American involvement in Vietnam just as one could bitterly resist *both* the Stalinist goon squads and Hitler's terrorists who were to clasp arms in fraternal concert a few years later. And even if this were not the case, as we easily can conceive it by changing the illustrations, the comparison is specious and question-begging to boot. Because we disapprove of violence in one context, say when extremists organize a riot to prevent a dialogue from taking place, we do not have to disapprove of it in another, say when those who believe in freedom fight to overthrow their oppressors. The assumption that all of these contexts are necessarily involved with one another will not stand examination for a minute.

The objection to violence in a democratic polity stems from various sources, not all of them narrowly political. The first reflects the civilized and humane belief that the amount of physical coercion of men over other men can be reduced although it cannot ever be eliminated. Even those who are wedded to violence as a strategy of social change profess to believe that their actions will produce a world that ultimately will be less violent. This is extremely unlikely, although not inconceivable either theoretically or practically. Tolstoy to the contrary notwithstanding, we *can* sometimes fight fire with fire and touch pitch without being defiled. But because of the interrelationship of means and ends, because the ends achieved depend not on the ends proclaimed but on the consequences of the means used, a very careful assessment of the probabilities is required before embarking on a course that entails much physical coercion.

Those who choose the democratic option whose institutions permit the minority peacefully to become the majority have presumably calculated the probabilities. Without accepting the argument of absolute pacifism, they recognize the pacifist insight that in using coercive force against the violent domestic and even foreign enemies of a democracy, there is always a danger that we may become like them. True, there is no world, there is no policy without its dangers. But the danger of the triumph of evil through nonresistance to evil is much greater than the danger that physical resistance to evil will result in a worse evil.

and predictability in their social life within the limits of what is humanly suffer-able. It is the certainty of law, the knowledge of what can be relied on as we go about arranging our affairs and tying them into the future, rather than our expectation that the delicate balance of justice will be precisely achieved in human relations, that is its chief desideratum. Violence, especially chronic vio-lence, upsets the normal expectations of orderly procedure. Unless a new pattern of stability is quickly reached an atmosphere of impending chaos and catastro-phe is generated that prepares the ground for the growth and tolerance of despotism. Despotism is not willingly or freely chosen. It comes when men become fearful of anarchy.

It is in the light of these considerations that we must examine what seems to be the most pervasive as well as the most persuasive argument for violence. This maintains that the threat of violence, and its actuality which is necessary to make the threat credible, are the most effective means of achieving reforms, that without the violent extremist the moderate reformer has no chance to imple-ment his program, that the prospects of reform are always enhanced by the fear generated through the threat of violence and its sporadic outbreaks. "Kill, burn, ravage!" exhorts the extremist leader. "Deal with me, or else face the irresponsi-bles," warns the moderate or reformist leader. His proposed compromises and concessions seem sweetly reasonable against the background of shrill cries of the mob. On this view it is only because of the multitudinous threats of violence emanating from plural pressure groups that keep each other in check that the democratic system works peacefully *on the whole*. But episodically and fitfully there must be outbreaks of violence to reinforce the readiness to be reasonable, to soften if not to dissolve the stubborn recalcitrance dug in to defend the sacred principles of the Establishment.

Without doubt there is some truth to this view. But it is a half-truth and a dangerous half-truth at that. From the abstract proposition that the threat or exercise of violence *may* facilitate enlightened social change or policy, it is the sheerest dogmatism to assume that in any particular situation violence or its threat will in fact serve a beneficial purpose. It may just as likely set up a cycle of escalating violence and counterviolence that will be more costly and undesira-ble than the reforms subsequently instituted. It all depends upon the case.

The theoretical basis of this position is purely Hobbesian with all its limita-tions. As one defender of this view put it: "In an important sense, all individuals, groups or nations desire 'to rule the world' but are constrained to collaborate with others on less desirable terms because of the objective limits of their own power."[5] In other words the chief, if not only, reason we bargain, tolerate, cooperate, live and let live with others is that we are not powerful enough to kill or enslave them. This is false not only for individuals but even for some states in some areas of the world and in some periods of history. Otherwise we could hardly explain the existence of small, relatively defenseless powers. And even

Hobbes recognized, as some of his modern descendants do not, that despite the hypothetical and largely mythical natural state of anarchy, once a community is established a binding commitment to resolve differences by due political process arises. For who would enter into a compact to surrender his power and abide by certain rules if every party to the compact added to it a rider that whenever it was strong enough to violate the rules with impunity, it would do so? If violence always, or even in most cases, paid, no social life could continue. It was realization of this that accounts for Hobbes' third law of nature, that "men perform their covenants made."

Turn from the dialectic of theory to the record of history. Is it true that the historical record proves that the fear or the actual outbreak of violence has been the sole or even the most important cause of reform? It would be a fantastic misreading of American history to assert this. Vast amounts of social welfare legislation for women, children, the aged, the sick and handicapped, the unemployed cannot be explained in terms of fear of violence. The motives and causes for their adoption are mixed, but among them an expanded social consciousness and sense of responsibility rank high. No one rioted for social security or Medicare or for the acceptance by the federal government of the revolutionary principle of a *national* minimum of welfare payments. Tremendous advances have been made in the defense and extension of civil rights and liberties, in judicial and penal practice, in the liberalization of laws relating to marriage, divorce, birth control, and abortion. All of these measures and many more have been adopted in the absence of any credible threats of violence. Not a single one of the great landmark decisions of the Supreme Court, including its outlawing of school segregation in 1954 and mandatory state political reapportionment a decade later, was made under the threat of the gun, the mob, or the torch. It is not to violence or the threat of violence that we owe their enactment, but to the growth of enlightenment, the enlargement of imagination, and the development of the democratic idea.

The view that only violence and the threat of violence can be effective in preparing the minds of men for change is in a sense worse than false. It is thoroughly confused. It does not distinguish between the effect of the fear that violence *may* break out and the effect of the actual violence *after* it has broken out, between the anticipatory fear and the consequential fear. There is no need to deny that fear of violence, but certainly not fear alone, does have an influence upon the willingness to reform conditions. And up to a point it is altogether reasonable that it should have an influence. Every society rests upon some shared values that determine acceptable and unacceptable, approved and disapproved norms of conduct. Basic in the hierarchy of such values is a shared interest in survival. Where conditions are so oppressive that those who live under them are tempted to a revolt that may encompass our common doom, self-interest legitimately reinforces the weight of ideals and human sympathy in motivating necessary reforms. An English writer once observed that "if we were all seated at the same table, no one would go hungry," and, I add, not because of fear but in virtue of the compassion that quickens the perception of need in others. We are indeed seated at the same table of life, but there are so many and they are so far away from us that those who are out of sight are out of mind too. Our imaginations are too weak and uncultivated to close the gap. Where vision falters, common sense, intelligent fear, may suggest a sensible course of conduct. If consideration for others does not lead to our extending to them the courtesy of the road, prudent fear for our own safety should. If the deficiencies of our imagination and moral feeling make us insensitive or indifferent to the plague, the poverty, the crime and degradation that flourish beyond our narrow horizons, then chill fear, born of the realization that these contagious evils—these diseases of body and spirit—may strike down our own children, may shake us out of our torpor into taking remedial action. Under such circumstances, intelligent fear, including fear that basic human needs long frustrated may erupt in violence, furthers cooperative effort.

Although *fear* of violence is often a persuasive reason among others for initiating reforms, this is not true to the same extent of overt, repeated *threats* of violence. And least persuasive of all is the brute outbreak of violence that imperils security of life, of one's home and property. For the consequence of such violence is the generation of hysteria and panic among its victims and all elements of the population who identify empathetically with them. This is particularly true when women and children are in the path of the violence.

Mass hysteria and panic are blind. They mistake fantasy for reality and breed unreasoning, not intelligent, fear and hate. If enough people among the majority are swept up in these emotions a reaction sets in, all the more intense for being delayed, that makes reforms more difficult to achieve, not less. It not only can stop the movement toward reform, it sometimes reverses it.

Whoever then calculates on the educational value of violence for the community, who anticipates that violence will strengthen the influence of moderates and expedite reform is taking a considerable risk, a foolish risk, and in the absence of compelling evidence that no other way is possible, a criminally irresponsible risk. He risks provoking a backlash, risks the hardening of opposition to further reforms, risks a counterviolence that as it escalates moves the conflict toward civil war, the cruelest form of all wars. In short, violence more often drowns out the voice of moderation than it succeeds in getting a hearing for it otherwise denied. It narrows options, destroys the center, and polarizes the community into extremes.

The American Civil War is a case in point. It did not solve the Negro question. We are still suffering from its legacy of hate and fear which left the Negro politically disfranchised, despite his legal emancipation as a war measure, economically in peonage, and socially and educationally victimized by a Jim

Crow system. It is still a moot question among historians whether at one time Lincoln's orginal plan of liberation of the slaves by purchase at a far lesser cost in life, money, suffering, and paranoic hatred would not have integrated the Negroes into American life more quickly and more effectively than did the Civil War. The prospects for the adoption of Lincoln's plan diminished to the vanishing point as the fanatics of violence on both sides heated regional consciousness to the boiling point.

What is not moot at all is the fact that since the Civil War the greatest gains in the condition of the Negroes in the United States were won not in consequence of violence or the threat of violence but by the use of democratic administrative and legal processes, fortified in recent times by the nonviolent civil rights movement headed by Dr. Martin Luther King. Civil disobedience, i.e., nonviolent disobedience, has a place, albeit not unrestricted, in a democratic community as a method of bearing moral testimony, of re-educating the majority and bringing it to second thoughts. Uncivil disobedience, i.e., violent disobedience, has no place whatsoever. The ghetto riots that periodically swept cities during the first three decades of this century brought no substantial reforms despite great loss of Negro life. Anyone who recalls the state of our country before the First World War will testify to the remarkable progress made since then—granted, of course, that this progress has still far to go to achieve the substantial equality to which all groups are entitled in a democratic community.

Roy Wilkins in defending the remarkable record of the NAACP in its unremitting militant but nonviolent struggle for Negro rights recently reminded a group of black extremists, impatient with its methods, that the victories won by the NAACP and other organizations of the Negro people had changed the political picture of the country, provided the opportunities for the extremists to be heard and to survive, and had laid the basis for still greater victories. He charged that white racism was responsible for the emergence of black racism. But he warned that black racism would result only in a stronger and subtler form of white racism. And he pleaded for the abolition of every form of racism in human relations.

What holds for the relationship between violence and reform with respect to the black citizens of the United States holds true even more obviously for the relationship between student violence and university reform. Some apologists for student violence maintain that it has led to necessary and healthy curricular and administrative reforms in the university. The wisdom of such reforms remains problematic where they were adopted not on the basis of sound educational inquiry but, as was frankly proclaimed in many institutions, as a means of keeping the campus quiet, of bringing peace to embroiled institutions. This is an extraordinary criterion by which to determine the validity of an educational curriculum.

Where the educational reforms mark essential improvements in instruction and administration, the crucial question to be decided is whether they would have been adopted if students had persistently agitated for them through the customary forms of dissent without threatening to tear the university apart or burn it down. The most significant feature of the student rebellion at Berkeley, at Columbia, at Harvard and elsewhere is that the grievances were not in the first instance connected with the students' own educational experience but with issues unrelated to curricular matters. Subsequently educational issues were moved to the forefront from the far periphery of student interest to outflank the devastating criticism of student irrationality in holding the university responsible for social and political involvements altogether beyond its sphere of competence and authority.

That *some* good results from violence does not justify the violence unless it can be proved that the good so achieved was necessary, could not have been achieved more effectively and at a lesser cost in other ways, and did not result in evil that outweighed the good. It is notorious that wars accomplish or rather result in some good—a great many advances in science, technology, and medicine have resulted from it. But only someone seriously deficient in compassion and imagination would therefore justify war. The truth of the matter is that most educational reforms in most institutions have come about *without* a show of force, where arguments have been the only weapons, where dissenters and protesters have evinced not only zeal but persistence in a good cause. Where violence has been used, a grievous wound has been inflicted on the fabric of university community life. It may take a generation to heal it. For the commitment of the university, even more so than of the democratic community, has always been to the processes of deliberation and to the authority of reason. Some faculty apologists for the student rebels have sought to play down the enormity of the offenses against intellectual and academic freedom by dismissing them as inconsequential. "Just a few buildings burned" they say, "some machines destroyed, a handful of classes disrupted, a dozen or so administrators and professors manhandled." This is as if one were to extenuate the corruption of justice by the numbers of magistrates not bribed, the desecration of a temple by the unusual character of the defilement, lynchings by their infrequency. The sober fact is that violence has reached such proportions on our campuses today that the whole atmosphere of American universities has been transformed. The appeal to reason is no longer sufficient to resolve problems or even to keep the peace. In order to make itself heard in some of our most prestigious institutions the appeal to reason must finally appeal to the courts and to the police.

Violence in the academy is an outgrowth of violence in the streets and cities of the country. That is where the gravest current danger lies. Were violence confined to the universities alone, its evils could not long continue if only because the state and society on whose support the universities ultimately depend would restrict and perhaps cancel their precarious autonomy. This could easily be done under the currently fashionable slogans of community control and participatory democracy in educational institutions.

In the democratic community at large the resort to violence, instead of reliance upon the due political process of a self-governing republic, attacks that community at its foundations. And this regardless of the merit of the cause or the sincerity and self-righteousness of the *engagés*. For every such outbreak of violence makes other outbreaks of violence more likely by serving as a model or precedent to some, or as a provocation to others—in either case escalating the violence.

In this connection Alexander Hamilton was truly prophetic. In the Federalist papers he warned us of this:

> Every breach of the fundamental law, though dictated by necessity, impairs that sacred reverence which ought to be maintained in the breast of rulers [who in a self-governing republic are all the people] towards the Constitution of the country, and forms a precedent for other breaches, where the same plea of necessity does not exist at all, or is less urgent and palpable.

Hamilton unerringly cited, on the basis of evidence from the past, the great danger of situations of this kind, the likelihood that citizens "to be more safe . . . at length become more willing to run the risk of becoming less free."

In the end, then, the great paradox and the great truth is that in a democratic society freedom, which is often invoked to justify violence, is itself imperiled by the exercise of violence. The ideologists of violence in a democracy are the sappers and miners of the forces of despotism, the gravediggers, witting or unwitting, of the heritage of freedom of the Western world.

A Climate for Change

Charles J. Hitch

Colleges and universities now are reputed to be fomenters of change, but they were far from friendly to it several hundred years ago. Indeed, their very reason for existence was the maintenance of the status quo. Their function was to train the future leaders of society—at first a society dominated by the church and later by the nation-state—and they did their job well. They passed on the accumulated knowledge of mankind along with a generous dose of dogma, religious and secular, and both church and state were well served.

Universities and their student bodies grew and, despite their essential conservatism, came into increasing conflict with their surrounding society. I quote from a small monograph entitled *Introduction to Cambridge*:

> Certainly by the year 1231 the body of Cambridge students was sufficiently important and sufficiently active to cause King Henry III to issue a number of writs for the punishment of disorderly scholars by the Sheriff, for the expulsion of students who were not under the direction of a master, and for the regulation of the rents of lodgings by two masters and two good and lawful men of the town. According to one historian, the troubles were provoked by a crew of pretenders to scholarship who lived under no discipline, having no tutor saving him who teaches all mischief.
>
> Town and gown riots were a common feature of the Middle Ages— strifes, fights, spoilings, breaking open of houses, woundings and murder twixt the burgesses and the scholars of Cambridge. . . .[1]

Somehow it is comforting to me to know that Henry III once shared my problems!

Much later, and principally in the German universities, the concept of research was developed as a primary mission of the university. Research was in a way subversive of universities because it sought deliberately after change, and change was incompatible with the basic conservatism of the institution. There was, in fact, a significant movement toward research institutes, and a separation of research from the older and more conservative mission of teaching. Once in the door, however, research stayed in the university, and the mission of research gradually attained equal stature.

The America university of the latter part of the nineteenth century added the third major mission of the modern university—public service—which assumes that the university has a responsibility to the society in which it exists and that society needs its ideas and imagination. Public service requires involvement instead of detachment and participation instead of scholastic aloofness, and it has changed the nature of the university and of society. So that brings us to the present, where teaching, research, and public service complement one another and universities are justifiably esteemed throughout the land. Well, not exactly. As a matter of fact, the missions of the university and the institution itself are being questioned all over the world.

The world, and particularly the United States, and perhaps most particularly California, are undergoing rapid, pervasive, and sometimes convulsive change. We are living astride a kind of social San Andreas Fault, and institutions, values, attitudes, and life styles are shaken. I might will it otherwise, but I am not surprised to find the role of the university also in flux.

I would like to discuss two interpretations of what a university's role should be; there are, of course, many variations on these themes. The first concept has been around for some time, for it really is the old medieval notion of the university as a conservative institution. It generally stresses the teaching mission of the university at the expense of research and public service, and it would favor rather tight control over the curriculum to strengthen through knowledge a student's belief in his national and cultural heritage. This concept is passive, and order and stability are two of its key aspects.

The second concept is anti-order and anti-stability, for it sees society as sick and badly in need of radical surgery. It would inflate the public-service mission of the university and transform the institution into an active, partisan agent of change. It, too, would control the curriculum, for it would channel all the institution's energies into what it would consider socially useful areas.

I hope it is obvious that both of these interpretations have serious flaws and that both of them would do violence to what a university should be. But both interpretations have one common flaw. Both reach a point where certain ideas are proscribed, certain opinions are banned, certain otherwise lawful activities are prohibited as dangerous to the university community. I believe the reverse is true, for I believe that the danger to the university—and indeed to the society at large—increases with every move toward restricting what may be talked about.

I realize that I am about to enter a tangled thicket, but I think a discussion of academic freedom will help me make my point. I wish, however, that we somehow could discuss the concept without using the term itself, for the term academic freedom has come to be a symbol which possesses a peculiar power to inflame the passions. You have probably noticed that there aren't very many persons who are undecided about academic freedom. To most faculty members it is the most divine of rights, and to a growing portion of the public it is a cloak for all kinds of evil activity.

The concept is actually very simple. It holds that to be effective—to be worthy of the name—a university *must* be open to the expression of all views, no matter how popular or how unpopular. It judges a faculty member by his intellectual capacity and his commitment to the free pursuit of learning. It does not, to be specific, punish a man because he privately opposes the war, or because he examines socialism in the classroom, or because he is a member of the John Birch Society. Freedom of thought and expression is what academic freedom is all about, and it cannot be compromised without compromising the university itself, and, indeed, the society.

I am afraid, however, that many people outside of the university—and a few within our community—believe that academic freedom is an unlimited license given to the faculty member to do anything he pleases. This is, of course, nonsense. Nothing is unlimited, and academic freedom is no exception. For example, a faculty member is not free to indoctrinate his students or to impose his ideas on them, for the students, too, have a kind of academic freedom—the freedom to learn. In addition, a faculty member must be careful to make clear that his private opinions are just that, his private opinions and not those of the university.

Academic freedom really is synonymous with integrity—the integrity of the professor, protected from those who would dictate his thoughts and actions, and the integrity or basic honesty of the professor when dealing with his students and with his institution. Academic freedom can be abused from many sides—from politicians, from regents, from students, and from the faculty itself. Like anything else worth having, it takes a lot of hard work to keep it.

We—and I mean all of us—must keep trying to preserve freedom of expression and freedom of inquiry, not merely because they sound good as abstract ideals but because they are vital to a healthy university and to a healthy society. We must be free to explore the fringes of our knowledge, to produce new knowledge, to develop new ways of thinking, and it is essential that all points of view be represented in a university, not necessarily *on* the faculty, but certainly *by* the faculty. You and I might agree that many of the views and ideas produced in such a free forum are worthless, or nonsensical, or perhaps even heretical. But dare we define what is permissible and what is not? Dare we take the chance of eliminating the creative and the positive along with what we might subjectively consider to be negative and destructive? I don't think the risk is worth it. I think rather that we should take a different kind of risk, the risk of exposure to ideas we don't like, the risk implicit in Justice Holmes' words about free trade in ideas. Holmes said:

> ... that the ultimate good desired is better reached by free trade in ideas—that the best test of truth is the power of the thought to get itself accepted in the competition of the market.[2]

I think the university must remain a marketplace of ideas, that our best chance for effecting positive change is contained in the promise of that marketplace, and that the risk of society's being seduced by a bad bargain there is very low. Moreover, we must have this freedom in order to sustain the creative role that a scholarly community must play if it is to be a university and not just a school.

Historically, the pressures to conform, to limit curricula, and to restrict and censor ideas and opinions have come from outside the university community. This sort of pressure is still with us and is understandable, for both individuals and societies become comfortable with the status quo and resent change, and some of this resentment is directed at universities as centers of change. But there is today a significant movement *within* universities toward conformity, and this is both new and particularly threatening, for this pressure on behalf of a new and rigid status quo, ironically enough, is made in the name of change itself.

Many of you are probably familiar with the button craze and you may have seen the button which reads:

If it feels good, do it.

Now, I admit that this slogan may have interesting social possibilities, but I am troubled by its logic, for I feel that this kind of thinking has led to a philosophy which on a button might read:

If you feel it *strongly* enough, it's true.

Thus, subjectivity would replace objectivity, opinion would replace fact, emotion replace reason, and the strength of voice supplant strength of argument. The ends come to justify the means, and any tactic is appropriate when the cause is just. Belief somehow becomes translated into fact, and the true believers feel it their duty to make converts by any means necessary. So in colleges and universities classrooms are disrupted in the name of education, speakers are shouted down in the name of free speech, job recruiters are driven from the campus in the name of morality, and demands for total conformity to a particular line of thought are made in the name of nonconformity and dissent.

This is wrong. If it is wrong for one group to seek to limit freedom of expression, it is wrong for another. Dogma is dogma, and it does not belong in a university, regardless of its origin and regardless of how many people agree with it.

If I abhor the trend toward a new conformity, I can understand how it has come about. We are living in frustrating times and they are perhaps particularly frustrating to the young. The problems—like war, race, and pollution—seem always to grow larger, not smaller, and there is a feeling of helplessness about it all. One recent survey shows that two-thirds of our young people agree at least in part that "America is unjust, inhumane, and insensitive," and they feel that there is little they can do to change it. The feeling is well expressed by Paul Goodman:

> Our psychology, in brief, is that history is out of control. It is no longer something that we make but something that happens to us.

That, really, should be the subject of another speech; so suffice it to say that there is more than a little justification for the current mood among young people, and I share some of their concerns.

However, I am also concerned that the nation seems to be growing more and more divided when we are so badly in need of cooperative effort. The threats of conformity hang over the nation as well as over the university, and the national climate for change is becoming poisoned. I think it is time to move beyond merely recognizing that there is alienation on our campuses and in our society, and to do something about it. We need a new reconciliation, and we need it soon. In this spirit, I want to share with you a poem by Robert Frost, "A Time to Talk."

> *When a friend calls to me from the road*
> *And slows his horse to a meaning walk,*
> *I don't stand still and look around*
> *On all the hills I haven't hoed,*
> *And shout from where I am, "What is it?"*
> *No, not as there is a time to talk.*
> *I thrust my hoe in the mellow ground,*
> *Blade-end up and five feet tall,*
> *And plod: I go up to the stone wall*
> *For a friendly visit.* [3]

Let us create on the campuses and in the country a new feeling, a new climate for change. Let us take the time to talk to one another, and let us respond with concern.

Moral Imperatives for Peace
In the Remainder of This Century

William G. Pollard

The moral and ethical imperatives for peace which stand out with urgency for the remaining years of this century are determined by the radical transformation through which the human species must go in this period. This transformation in turn is the consequence of the massive increase in human population which will occur over the next thirty years with its attendant problems of overcrowding, urban concentration, waste accumulation and pollution, and dwindling resources. One cannot deal meaningfully with the moral imperatives with which the future will present us without first dealing with this context within which they will be defined.

For the first time in history men everywhere are beginning to sense that their planet, the earth, is finite, small, and limited in its capacity to support them. We have seen the earth from the perspective of the Apollo missions and we can all now visualize it, as we have never really been able to before, as it really is: a beautiful but small ball floating in the vastness of space. We no longer think of it, as did men in all earlier centuries, as an unending frontier, unlimited in extent and resources and providing without end new opportunities for man to progress to ever higher and higher levels of achievement and development. Instead we have in just the last few years begun to become increasingly alarmed by premonitions of disaster in man's relationship to a shrinking planet. All over the earth we are running out of fresh water and food. We are conscious of the rapid deterioriation of the environment, the dangerous levels to which air and water pollution have risen, and the staggering annual increases in the accumulation of solid wastes. We have begun to question whether the earth is big enough and rich enough to hold us much longer.

The primary source of all these concerns is the explosive increase in the population which is peculiar to this century. It was only a short forty years ago, in 1930, that the total number of human beings on the planet reached 2 billion. It now stands at over 3.5 billion. By 1975 we will number 4 billion, and sometime between 1985 and 1989 we will reach 5 billion. By the end of the century, just thirty years from now, we will number between 6 and 7 billion and the earth will be twice as crowded as it is now. A mammoth effort sustained year by year in tropical agriculture and in related agro-industry and food transportation will be required to avert catastrophic famines in tropical Central and South America, Africa, the Middle East, Southeast Asia, and Mainland China. Immense new sources of fresh water must be found and developed. An enormous increase in the production of petroleum, metals, and fertilizers will be needed. Massive efforts to cope with pollution, waste disposal, and environmental deterioration must be mounted. Moreover all this must be accomplished within a political context involving social paroxysms of gravely increasing intensity as we crowd together on the planet.

The first chapter of Genesis ends with a summary of what God intended and accomplished when he brought man to this planet. "So," it says by way of summary, "God created man in his own image and he blessed them and said to them, be fruitful and multiply and fill the earth and subdue it, and have dominion over the birds of the air, and over the fish of the sea, and over the cattle, and over the whole earth." This summary is in a sense a key to the twentieth century. In this century alone among the hundreds that man has inhabited the planet it will have been fulfilled. At the start of the century none of it was true of man and the earth. By the end of the century it will all have been fulfilled. The earth will be full of the species Homo sapiens. He must either learn how to stop being fruitful and further multiplying his numbers or leave it to starvation and disease to prevent his further increase. By means of his science and technology he will have effectively subdued the whole planet to his purposes and taken dominion over all other creatures together with the entire resources of the planet in minerals, fossil fuels, land, water, and air. The earth will have been converted into the spaceship it perhaps was intended to be all along for carrying this last major creation of a long evolutionary history on this endless journey through space.

It is, it seems to me, this fulfillment of man's destiny on the planet which is now coming so rapidly upon us which defines the moral imperatives which must increasingly dominate the remainder of the century. The industrial revolution has been under way less than two hundred years. So far it has been conducted in a way which in no sense politically, socially, or economically has recognized this spaceship status of man on the planet. To realize this, we have only to ask the question of the attitude and practice of the crew of a spaceship with respect to the supply and quality of air and water in their ship, the means of food production, waste processing and disposal, conservation and utilization of limited reserves of energy and materials, and interpersonal relations among crew members throughout their space voyage. In none of these respects have we treated the earth as our spaceship. Yet the dynamics of social and economic change during the last third of this century will of necessity, independently of our desires and ambitions, force upon us this drastic reorientation in man's relationship to his planet.

This fact will define the moral imperatives that will force themselves upon mankind as a whole, slowly at first in the seventies, but more and more insistently in the eighties and nineties. As I visualize these imperatives they group themselves into two broad categories. One could be called the moral imperatives of the Commons and the other the moral imperatives of scarcity. It is these areas which will mainly concern me in this presentation. I am aware that there are many others of a more immediate concern. For the sixties they center around such issues as the nuclear arms race, the worldwide problem of racism, ideological conflicts between the communist and capitalist world. These have been dealt with at length by others. In failing to treat them at any length I do not ignore or belittle them, but rather choose to discuss aspects not otherwise extensively treated which seem of central importance for the future.

MORAL IMPERATIVES OF THE COMMONS

My terminology and many of my ideas in this section are based on a paper which appeared in the journal *Science*[1] nearly a year ago. It was written by Garret Hardin, a professor of biology at the University of California at Santa Barbara, under the title "The Tragedy of the Commons" with the subtitle "The population problem has no technical solution; it requires a fundamental extension in morality." It is a highly significant paper and it defines a moral imperative which must increasingly dominate our corporate life on the planet as we approach the point of filling it.

The Commons represent all portions of the planet which mankind as a whole, or at least large but definable social subgroups, use, or will increasingly come to use, in common. Examples for the whole of mankind are the high seas, the atmosphere, the space beyond the atmosphere, the planetary supply of fresh water over the land areas of the earth, and the reserves of metallic ores, petroleum, natural gas, sulfur, and phosphorus in the earth's crust. Examples of Commons shared by definable subgroups are national parks, highways, the Great Lakes, airways, ocean beaches, and the like.

Until relatively recently the moral dimensions of the shared use of the earth's Commons did not arise in any particularly acute or obvious form. As long as the total human population was small and the Commons essentially unlimited and adequate for the needs of all who desired to use them, the morality of the Commons did not arise. It is only as the number of people using them increases and the capacity of all the earth's Commons to satisfy human desires becomes more and more limited, that this kind of moral imperative arises. This has happened rapidly in many areas today. Let us consider a few basic examples and then, in terms of these, attempt to define the character of the moral imperatives involved.

1. *Science*, vol. 162 (13 December 1968), 1243-48.

Under the pressure of mounting world food requirements, the harvest of food from the sea is showing a dramatic growth rate. In the century from 1850 to 1950 the world catch from the oceans increased tenfold, at an average rate of 25 percent per decade. In the last decade it has nearly doubled to a present catch of about 55 million metric tons per year. Three quarters of the total harvest is taken by 14 countries whose catch exceeds 1 million tons. Of these, some of the major harvesters are Peru, the Soviet Union, Japan, and Norway. The United States has remained fairly constant for many years with an average catch of about 2 million tons per year.

Our scientific knowledge of the web of life in the sea involving ocean currents in relation to food nutrients, light intensity and photosynthesis, and the chain of feeding from plankton to large fish has increased greatly in the last two decades. We can now delineate the high food-producing regions of the seas and the kind of harvests which will lead to an optimum utilization of the food-producing capacity of the oceans. For each species in each region there is an optimum catch which produces the maximum amount of food protein with a minimum reduction in marine populations. If this optimum were followed, it is estimated that the harvest of food from the seas could be quadrupled to around 200 million metric tons per year. But if over-fishing occurred, species would be rapidly reduced in numbers toward extinction in a few years and the optimum harvest correspondingly reduced in tonnage.

Presently there are more than twenty established organizations under bilateral or multilateral treaties, or under the constitution of the Food and Agriculture Organization, designed to limit over-fishing. These are supplemented by the 1958 Geneva Convention on Fishing and Conservation of the Living Resources of the High Seas. These organizations are poorly supported and, so far, have largely been failures in achieving the objectives for which they were established. There are already a number of examples of severe losses resulting from failure of national fishing fleets and even individual fleets of the same nation to follow optimum practice. The improper management in the capture of cod in the North Atlantic and of salmon in the Northeastern Pacific alone represents a loss of 5 percent in the total world catch of all types of fish. Failure to introduce and enforce mesh regulations in the Central Atlantic off the West Coast of Africa for mainly hake fishing is resulting in an annual loss of 1 million dollars. Failure to regulate the Antarctic whaling industry in earlier years when numbers of blue whales and fin whales were near optimum is now costing tens of millions of dollars annually. Even under stringent regulations now imposed, this loss will continue for several decades before these stocks can recover to optimum numbers. Similar exploitation has occurred in the case of yellowfin tuna in the tropical Pacific.

In spite of these facts, little progress is being made in the search for effective international controls. Annual quotas should be established for each species, but how are the quotas to be divided among nations? On the basis of national catches over the last two years, five years, or twenty years? On the basis of population or food nneds? Or, in place of species quotas, should the number and tonnage of vessels be established for each species? If so, what flags should the ships fly and in what proportion? How do new nations not previously represented develop a marine harvesting potential? For any of these problems, what agency will police agreements and how can reliable inspection be carried out? These and a host of other questions beset this problem. No matter how much we know, or will come to know, of the scientific and technical aspects of producing food from the sea, none of that knowledge will help us at all in resolving these questions.

These questions highlight the basic moral dilemma which is characteristic of all situations involving Commons. For the individual fishing vessel one more catch adds a full 100 percent in value. This is balanced on the deficit side of the ledger by its effect on the total marine population of the species caught, which at the optimum level may be only a tiny fraction of one percentage point. On the other hand, the greater the extent of over-fishing and the tighter the squeeze on marine resources, the greater is the suspicion of all fishermen that the others are not abiding by the regulations, and the greater becomes the incentive for each fisherman to flout them.

Another Commons is the atmosphere and fresh water systems of the earth which presently are of such grave concern in terms of pollution. Here too the individual sources of pollution are many and diverse. Every operator of a motor vehicle, every family unit in an apartment or house, every power plant and chemical industry, and every farmer who uses soluble fertilizer on his land or insecticides on his crops is a contributor to either air or water pollution or both. For each one, the moral dilemma of the Commons holds. To halt his share of the pollution would represent a sizeable outlay whose effect on his own resources he counts as a large percentage. Failure to do so, on the other hand, continues to contribute to the total volume of pollutants only a minute fraction of one percentage point of the total. Confronted with such a tremendous imbalance between his own loss and the minuscule gain for the environment, the individual feels that he must have complete assurance that the system of controls will guarantee that every other individual will suffer, for the common good, a loss equivalent to his own. Otherwise he can only conclude that social pressure, and perhaps his own conscience, are manipulating him into the position of playing the fool for a cause in which few others are supporting him.

These and all other problems of the Commons arise basically as a result of a single primary cause—too many people. It is the fact of man's filling the earth in this century which generates them all. Thus the population of our species on the planet itself becomes the primary Commons for mankind with respect to which all other Commons are secondary. The primary problem for the remainder of this century is first to stop our population increase and then to slowly reduce it to a level which the earth can support. The accomplishment of this objective, however, presents the moral dilemma of the Commons in its most acute form. Each family unit which decides to have one additional child must enter in their ledger a gain to them of +1 and a loss to the achievement of society's objective of -1/4,000,000,000th. With such odds to contend with, a man and wife can only conclude that, unless they are persuaded that all other couples are abstaining so that they alone stand out as culprits, their act involves an insignificant damage to society as a whole. How this dilemma is to be resolved is a question of almost impossible difficulty, yet its resolution represents perhaps the primary moral imperative of the remainder of the century.

As population increases all over the world, many lesser questions involving the morality of the Commons will arise. One example which touches my own personal experience is that of national parks. When our great national parks were first established in this country, they were reserves of magnificent natural beauty, preserved so far as possible in their pristine state for the enjoyment of all who wished to visit them. But our growing population and greater leisure are resulting each year in greatly increased numbers of people visiting each of our parks. The result is a steady erosion of the values which each visitor seeks in a park. Ultimately we must somehow cease to treat the parks as Commons or they will not be of any value to anyone. As one who from boyhood has derived great spiritual benefit and deep enjoyment from protracted hikes into the silent and majestic fastnesses of the Great Smoky Mountains, I have in recent years become acutely aware of this threat. I ask myself how much of my own development, or that of my sons, as a full human person would have been stunted if I had not had this opportunity? When I observe what is happening to that particular national park, I wonder whether the generations to come will have any such opportunities left on the earth.

This problem reveals in a microcosm the moral dilemmas inherent in all Commons as man fills the earth. Quite obviously it is an area of morality, i.e., of the sphere of what we ought to do in contrast to what in fact we do do, which cannot be left to the individual conscience but must be dealt with corporately. The preservation of the original purpose for which the parks were established demands some means of limiting the number of visitors to them. This could be by means of steeper and steeper admission charges, on a merit basis as a reward for public service, by a lottery system, on a first-come-first-served basis, or some other equally objectionable plan. But, however objectionable, there is no other alternative for this or any of the other Commons of the earth. The continued unregulated access to all of them which is now permitted, including individual freedom to add to the population of our species on the planet at will, can only destroy the value of all Commons for every individual. During the remainder of this century this moral problem can only grow in importance as an absolute imperative for our continued occupation of the planet.

THE MORALITY OF SCARCITY

The second moral imperative which confronts us starkly as we look toward the future has to do with our management and stewardship of the earth's limited natural resources. Until recently this question was hardly ever raised, except by a very limited number of isolated voices which went essentially unheeded. Today the problem is being much more widely discussed than it was just a few years ago, and it is bound to receive much wider attention as the century advances to its close. Even now, however, the moral aspects of the problem are rarely if ever acknowledged. It is this area which I would like to discuss next as the other moral imperative of fundamental importance which confronts us in the remaining three decades of this century.

The industrial revolution is not yet two centuries old. We can date its beginning at about 1790 when the first steam engines began to be manufactured and put to practical use based on James Watt's earlier discovery. Its course in the intervening 180 years has been a remarkable record of accelerating change which by now has profoundly modified the whole status of man on the planet. In practically all discussions of man's future it is taken as axiomatic that this change is a permanent one. The industrial-technological society is axiomatically taken to be here to stay. In this century it is being extended to all portions of the world; to the so-called "underdeveloped" countries, which had not previously experienced it. We look confidently forward to the time when technology with all its fruits, comforts, and leisure time will have clothed the whole planet. Thereafter mankind will settle down to the universal enjoyment of affluence for all the rest of time. This is the kind of projection from our present situation that people have in mind when they talk about the new age of space travel, of supersonic transport, of automation or computers, or of transplants and artificial organs in medicine. It is a vision of unending progress in which what we have experienced so far is merely the first taste of what the new world will be universally like. Look, they say, at what has happened to air travel in just the last forty years. In another forty years, space travel to the moon and the planets will have become just as common. Or consider the immense changes which we have all experienced in just the last twenty years as a result of the computer, in the development of programmed control systems by fully automating production processes and routine clerical and business functions. Surely this is only the beginning of a process which can only go forward to the accomplishment of ever larger and more complex tasks.

It is my thesis here that this vision of endless technological progress and universal technological application simply cannot be. Rather than representing a permanent transformation in man's status on the planet, I believe the industrial revolution will be seen in the retrospect of the twenty-first century and after to have been a brief and profligate joy ride of no more than two centuries' duration—a fleeting incident in the long history of man and his planet. In saying this I do not mean that we shall then simply return to the non-scientific agrarian society of the eighteenth century. History never simply returns to previous epochs. It will continue to be a sophisticated scientific-technological society. But it will be one dominated by scarcity, not affluence, and characterized by retrenchment, not progress and expansion.

We see now that there are three essential ingredients in the industrial revolution. The first is energy, as symbolized by the steam engine which started it but now expanded to include the internal combustion engine, the electric motor, jet engines and rockets, and nuclear power plants. The second is human ingenuity and inventiveness, symbolized at first by the great inventors such as Watt, McCormick, Edison, and Bell, and later by science applied by organized teams of experts in mammoth laboratories and symbolized by such things as nylon, plastics, radar, atomic energy, transistors, and lasers. The third is a vast reservoir of resources readily available for every application with abundant supplies of water, coal, petroleum, natural gas, iron, copper, aluminum, lead, phosphate, nitrogen, cement, sulfur, and many others. All three of these are essential to the scientific-technological society that we so confidently project indefinitely into the future. The collapse of any one of them would bring down the entire enterprise. It is this simple consideration which lies at the heart of my thesis.

The industrial revolution started with a simple combination of these three elements: steam energy from coal, the invention of Watt, and metallic iron. Compared to all previous epochs of man's history, the demand for iron was immense. There were the steam engines themselves, the increasingly complicated machinery they drove, rails for the railroads, etc. But to meet this need in this country there was the inexhaustible supply of rich, up to 80 percent, iron ore in the Mesabi Range in Minnesota—literally mountains of such ore. Thus began our steadily mushrooming iron and steel industry. By the start of this century the stage was set for the evolution of the modern industrial society. One after another came the telegraph, the telephone, the automobile, and electric lights and motors. All these developments led to an enormous production of goods based essentially on cheap coal for power, available for the digging of it, and on cheap and abundant iron and copper available to all who would simply mine it out of the ground. As American industry grew there was always plenty of power to run it, plenty of raw material to feed it, and plenty of ideas from a smart and resourceful people to develop it to ever-increasing levels of complexity. Machines were developed to produce other machines in a hierarchy of growing complexity involving machines to obtain the raw materials, machines to fabricate them into products, machines to build railroads and highways, machines to transport other machines, in a new and endless sequence. The result is an immense, enormously complex and interlocking system of mines, factories, farms, cities, and transportation and communication facilities.

In the development of this intricate organism every new idea has been able to assume without question the availability of the raw materials needed to carry it out, and every new product placed on the market could obtain all the raw materials needed for its mass production. But we stand now on the threshold of a new era in which the previously taken-for-granted condition will increasingly fail to exist any longer. By the end of the century shortages of many of the raw materials of the industrial society will have become acute. This will mean vast changes in the outlook which many now take for granted, and a radical readjustment for all mankind in our relationship to the planet which sustains us. Such a readjustment will bring with it new moral imperatives of a scope and depth which few today suspect. The moral issues which confront us today are shaped by the affluent society. Those which we shall face tomorrow will increasingly be shaped by scarcity.

One resource has already become scarce. That is fresh water. The average person drinks about 200 gallons of water annually. In addition to this he requires about 15,000 gallons of water annually for bathing, cooking, laundering, lawn watering, and heating and air-conditioning equipment. These quantities are dwarfed by industry, which for making gasoline, paper, cloth, steel, chemicals, and many other things requires 160,000 gallons of water per year for every person. Irrigation of our farms to grow our food requires some 250,000 gallons per person per year and this amount will greatly increase as the century advances and more and more people need to be fed. Over 90 percent of the domestic and industrial water is returned to streams, lakes, or the ocean combined with vast quantities of industrial wastes, noxious chemicals, excreta, and other pollutants.

All over the world we are running out of fresh water. We have the technology in hand to obtain it, even for double the present population in another thirty years, provided we are willing to invest vast quantities of energy to obtain it. We can divert to inland deserts some of the immense but useless flow into the Arctic Ocean which now occurs in Canada and Siberia through the Yukon, Mackenzie, Ob, Yenisei, and Lena rivers. Along coastal deserts we can desalt the sea with immense nuclear-powered evaporators, In some places, such as the Ganges valley in India and Pakistan, we can pump water out of great subterranean reservoirs. With sufficient energy we can depollute the water from municipal and industrial effluents and reuse it for other purposes downstream. All this can be done but only at great cost in energy and dollars.

The next resource to go will be petroleum and natural gas. At mid-century over 70 billion barrels of petroleum had been removed from the earth, almost all of it since 1900. In 1967 United States consumption was 3.7 billion barrels per year and was rising rapidly. Total world consumption stood at 13 billion barrels per year. The combination of economic development throughout the underdeveloped world with population increases everywhere indicates a fivefold increase in worldwide average consumption to something like 60 billion barrels annually over the twenty years between 1970 and 1990. This means the withdrawal of more than a trillion barrels from the earth during that period. In 1967 the known world reserves amounted to some 60 billion barrels in North and South America, 35 billion barrels in Eastern Europe and the Soviet Union, and 210 billion barrels in the Middle East. Scattered reserves of 25 billion barrels elsewhere raised the known world reserves to 325 billion barrels. Additional large reserves in Arctic Alaska are just now being opened up, and similar ones can be expected in Arctic Canada and Siberia. The continental shelves are another future source provided oil can be safely extracted from deep-sea wells. Perhaps all of this may amount to double the known reserves. The absolute total reserve in the earth is of course unknown but it is certainly limited. We know a great deal about the geology of petroleum and there are not likely to be many surprises in store on the location of large new reserves. All indications at present are that probably by the early nineties and certainly by the end of the century natural petroleum production will be approaching its end.

Again, with a sufficient allocation of energy and dollars we can still have gasoline and jet fuel for our aircraft. We can make it out of coal plus hydrogen from the electrolysis of sea water. When the coal is gone, we can even make it out of carbon dioxide from air plus hydrogen from water at a cost of from four to six dollars a gallon. But before this century ends we will not have any more of it from oil or natural gas which we simply take out of the ground for the asking.

Iron is not yet as critical as these other resources. In the United States the mountains of iron ore we possessed in the Mesabi Range earlier this century are all gone and in their place is a vast hole in the earth like the Grand Canyon. We are now processing Lake Superior taconites, which run from 25 to 35 percent iron in place of the 60 to 70 percent ore we used up to the mid-1940s. Reserves of this ore in the United States amount to some 120 billion long tons. Elsewhere in the world sizable reserves of 40 to 70 percent ore still exist in Australia, Brazil, Canada, Europe, and India, with the largest, in the Soviet Union, amounting to some 90 billion long tons.

The United States imports about a third of the iron ore used in our domestic production. Presently that production amounts to some 130 million tons of iron and steel per year. The total amount of iron and steel presently in use in the United States is about 15 tons per person. Because of rust and other nonrecoverable losses, it was necessary to produce over 20 tons per person to have this much left. If the whole world were to come up to U.S. standards of economic development by the year 2000 and there were then 6 billion people in it, we would have to produce another 100 billion tons of iron and steel in the next 30 years. This of course is not at all likely to happen, but it shows that such a standard would easily exhaust all of the earth's resources of ores with 25 percent iron content or better. Even on the most optimistic estimates, such ores could not produce much more than 100 billion tons of iron and steel.

Three important resources—mercury, tin, and helium—are already very close to depletion. Certain other vital metals such as copper, lead, chromium, and manganese are much closer to depletion than is iron. One of the oldest in human use is copper, and it remains one of the most vital now. In the eighteenth century, ores with less than 13 percent copper were considered impractical. By the 1950s we were processing ores under 1 percent copper. The Materials Resources Commission set up by President Truman reported then that it was impractical to process copper ores of less than 0.5 percent copper. The total world reserve of ores of this copper content or better is under 200 million tons and world production exceeds 6 million tons per year. As the price of the metal has gone above fifty cents per pound, an increasing amount of this production is from recovered scrap. Rising economic development and world population increase will probably exhaust the world supply of all ores above 0.5 percent copper by sometime in the 1980s. After that we can still get copper, but again at very high costs in energy and dollars.

Other metals whose moderately low-grade ores are likely to be exhausted by 1990 are lead, chromium, and manganese. Some uses, such as tetraethyl lead in gasoline, are by nature nonrecoverable. Chromium is essential for stainless steel. Manganese is used in a nonrecoverable way in steel production, and the major remaining world supply is in the Soviet Union.

I know of no analysis of the implications of this situation such as the one that I wish to develop here. It is my contention that the exhaustion of natural resources of fresh water, petroleum, natural gas, and even medium-grade ores of many vital metals by the last decade of this century inevitably means the end of the industrial revolution as we have known it in this century, and certainly the end of affluence and the beginning of the age of scarcity. This implication is obscured by arguments which show that in each individual instance we can overcome the lack of a good natural resource with sufficient energy and expense, or with the development of cheaper substitutes. The development of nuclear power and the near assurance of efficient breeder reactors which can reconstitute the fuel they burn by breeding nonfissionable uranium and thorium, and generate power at half present costs is a shining and realizable hope. Such a development will make it possible for us to cope with any one of these failing resources we choose. But no one to my knowledge has put all of these needs together at once and then tried to visualize a solution even with cheap and abundant nuclear energy.

Consider first the normal rate of increase in power demands for the existing situation in the world, simply projected from past trends in the last ten years and based on expected increases in population and rates of economic development in underdeveloped countries for the next twenty years. Superimpose on this basic demand the additional power requirements over the next twenty years for dealing with pollution. We are just beginning to seriously tackle corrections for a rapidly deteriorating environment through measures to rigorously control emissions into the atmosphere, finance municipal sewage treatment facilities, regulate industrial and agricultural water pollution, and dispose of growing mountains of solid wastes. All this will require staggering increases in electric power and power machinery in the next twenty years. On top of this add the immense amount of power required to supply necessary irrigation water and fertilizer, particularly ammonia, to cope with the world food problem in this same period. To all these requirements must then be added the large additional blocks of power to hydrogenate coal for liquid fuel to replace petroleum, to make steel, aluminum, and magnesium for massively increasing demands for structural materials, and to win copper, chromium, and lead from the extremely lean ores which will be all that are left in the earth twenty years from now. A total energy picture constructed in this way, as opposed to isolated energy requirements for particular tasks, is staggering indeed.

My own judgment is that this total energy requirement simply cannot be met, not for technological reasons but from practical, political, and economic considerations. New nuclear power plants are already meeting strong public resistance from conservationists concerned with thermal pollution, radioactive contamination, and accidental hazards. Much of this is based on erroneous information and will, I am confident, be overcome because in the end people will not do without electricity, and the transportation and jobs dependent on it, in order to avoid insults to the environment and risks which are much more emotional than real. But on the really major scale of energy expansion we are considering here, thermal pollution from nuclear or any kind of power does become a limiting factor. So too does the requirement of capital investment, power transmission, chromium for stainless steel, availability of cooling water, and many other factors. On a worldwide, planetary scale which includes all requirements in a balanced whole, energy simply cannot ultimately counteract the effects on the economy as a whole of dwindling natural resources. Our plight would be truly desperate if it were not for the early prospect for cheap and abundant nuclear energy. That prospect insures the possibility of man's survival on the planet, although not the survival of that unnecessarily luxurious and profligate squandering of resources which we call the age of affluence.

Few have realized the extent to which the affluent society which we all take so much for granted has been generated by the wide and easy availability of rich natural resources and a limited population to enjoy them. Our world of two-car households, pleasantly heated and air-conditioned houses and offices, manifold electrical appliances and power tools, rapid jet transport, superhighways, color TV, and all the rest has been created out of an exploitation of those resources. As the resources dwindle and the wastes and pollution arising from their profligate exploitation grow, that world must go. None of the desperate measures dependent on energy or substitute materials which many count upon to save it can really rescue it. We will have cheap and abundant energy and many substitutes for scarce materials. But by the two-hundreth anniversary of the industrial revolution in 1990 the present affluent society it has made possible will already be vanishing. The human species will have had two centuries of marvelous luxury in a magic garden. Thereafter for the rest of time it must adjust itself to the hard realities of life outside the garden.

For the most part the transformation will not be planned or carried out by edict. The complex interplay of factors which constitutes "the economy" in either capitalist or communist countries will actually carry it out. The entire system is too complex and too delicately interconnected for anyone to foresee just how the adjustments will be made. The result must, however, allocate increasingly scarce materials more and more to essential purposes the foremost of which is certainly food production. One can foresee a time near the end of this century or early in the next when an automobile will cost the average person a year's salary to purchase and a tenth of his annual income to operate. Most houses and apartments will be heated by waste heat from nuclear power plants, but automatic washing machines, home freezers, and air conditioners will be beyond the reach of most. Travel for pleasure and even for business will become more and more curtailed. Useless exploits which increasingly squander precious reserves of fuel and metal, such as space exploration, will finally be dropped entirely. Other adjustments can only be dimly guessed at.

Uncertainties about projected rates of consumption of various resources and discoveries yet to be made of new and unsuspected reserves make it impossible to predict just when any particular resource will have been effectively exhausted. Even if a maximum capital investment in new power plants is made, we cannot foresee exactly how priorities for this new power will be set between water for agriculture, waste processing and pollution control, metal and fertilizer production, and inner-city transportation networks. Over and above such considerations the great complexity and subtlety of what we call "the economy" prohibits any reliable visualization of its response to the shrinkage of particular resources, and even more so of several in combination, or their growing replacement with various substitutes. Most people with whom I have discussed this problem believe we will continue to find new sources, or develop adequate substitutes, or find some new scientific or technological twist to extricate us. They do not take seriously the picture I have drawn in the foregoing and refuse to believe that an end of affluence is even possible for at least several centuries. I know of no particular or detailed arguments which can be advanced to persuade them otherwise.

My thesis is made even more difficult to be taken seriously by the fact that for the next twenty years we probably will have all the petroleum, natural gas, copper, chromium, and most other materials we want. As long as they last the organization of modern economic systems insures that they will be used. Production is tied solely to demand, and will automatically keep up with demand as long as any resources remain for doing so. In this period primary attention will be concentrated on obtaining fresh water, producing and marketing enough food, and bringing the more serious insults to the environment under control. It will only be in the nineties that the age of affluence begins its abrupt end. By then the thesis I have advanced here will, I am convinced, have begun to be taken very seriously by large numbers of people.

Basically my argument simply rests on the proposition that our present affluent society with its phenomenal standard of living has been created by abundant resources widely and cheaply available to all who desired them. The removal of this resource base is certain to pull the rug out from under the affluent society. Just what will be done in specific instances or just how the economy will make adjustments to the dwindling of the base on which it is erected is impossible to predict. But it is predictable, I believe, that the joy ride we have been on in this century can last not much more than another twenty years. After that we have to contemplate a very different status of man on his planet than the one we have become so accustomed to. We will still have abundant energy and great ingenuity and scientific-technical know-how. We will be able to do almost any particular thing we want to do. But it will be simply impossible for us to continue to do simultaneously all of the things we want to do. Our hard choices of the few particular things we feel we must do, that is our priorities, will somehow have become translated into the prices we have to pay for the variety of things we will still want. By then it will be a very different economy than the one we know now in the affluent society. It will be an economy tailored to the requirements of the age of scarcity.

To many this will seem a very pessimistic outlook, but I do not intend it to be taken pessimistically. It all depends on the value one attaches to the affluence and high standard of living to which we have become accustomed in America in this century. Many of our more sensitive young people are in rebellion against the high value placed on these by their elders. For anyone who does not feel that the essence of the good life resides in automobiles, air conditioning, jet air transport, and other such technological blessings, it may even be an optimistic rather than a pessimistic outlook to contemplate the vanishing of that kind of material overplus to life. We will not be helpless in the age of scarcity. We will have great scientific and technological ingenuity and abundant energy with which to apply it to our problems. We will probably learn how to design and build liveable cities, and to provide adequate transportation for our real needs at a minimum expenditure of scarce materials per passenger. We can produce sufficient food and goods and services for our real needs, although not for the excessive and often unhealthy material desires we have created in this century. We will have learned to save for reprocessing every scrap of metal we use and we will have become accustomed again to a maximum use of returnable containers. None of this, however, necessarily implies human lives of lowered quality or diminished potential. If in fact the reverse is the case, so that the moral and spiritual quality of human life will be greatly improved, then the contemplation of the end of affluence is actually optimistic.

THE MORAL IMPERATIVES FOR PEACE

If one were to detail the moral imperatives for peace as they can be discerned from the experience of the sixties, they would doubtless include in a prominent position the overcoming of the threat of nuclear warfare, the eradication of racism, and the alleviation of communist-capitalist ideology as a dominant force in international tensions. All three will undoubtedly remain as major world problems throughout the seventies. Nevertheless, it is my conviction that they will not remain dominant in the form in which we now conceive them throughout the remainder of the century.

We have lived now for a quarter of a century under the continuous threat of nuclear catastrophe. We are quite likely to continue to live with this same threat in even graver forms for another quarter of a century at least. Yet, as has so often happened before in history, the catastrophe we dread the most may be the one which does not materialize while another catastrophe we do not expect will be the one which comes upon us. I have this feeling about nuclear warfare. There are doubtless several nations in the Middle East, Mainland China, Africa, and elsewhere which would not presently hesitate to use nuclear weapons if they possessed them and the means of their delivery in quantity. But by the time they had developed the sophisticated and widespread industrial complex essential for the quantity production of efficient nuclear weapons and an extensive deployment of long-range missiles with accurate inertial guidance systems to actually launch a nuclear war, they would feel very differently. By then they would necessarily have developed a vast complex of very sophisticated industries, suppliers of electronic components, and numerous auxiliary enterprises. Large numbers of highly trained and educated people would be involved in this system and an immense capital investment would have been made in bringing it into being. As this complex gradually came into being, there would inevitably grow beside it a large civilian industry in electric power, automobiles, modern housing, and the like. By the time such a nation was ready to launch missiles with nuclear warheads in any significant quantity, it would have become dominated by the desire to preserve and protect from destruction what it had put so much into building. At that stage it would never bring itself to the decision to launch its nuclear capability. We have already seen this built-in control in successful operation in the Cuban crisis. In spite of everything Khrushchev had at stake in that crisis in the way of national prestige and influence, as well as his own personal destiny, he nevertheless backed away from a decision to release the substantial nuclear capability he had at his command.

The real tragedy in the widespread development and deployment of both offensive and defensive nuclear warfare systems is the enormous squandering of precious and increasingly limited resources which it entails. During the first fifty years of this century the world as a whole spent four thousand billion dollars on arms and military operations. If present trends in the arms race continue, the world will spend the same amount in the seventies, equaling a short ten years the expenditure of half a century. Military expenditures for the world as a whole in 1967 amounted to 182 billion dollars and consumed 7 percent of mankind's entire production of goods and services in that year. This expenditure represents $53 per year for every man, woman, and child on earth.

A diversion of goods and services of this magnitude for military purposes involves a tremendous drain on the earth's natural resources. However necessary for its defense each nation may regard this drain, the end result is a complete diversion of those resources from the needs of individual human beings. As the age of affluence begins to come to an end in the nineties, the immense squandering of resources in this century will seem a cruel blow. This will be particularly true of resources diverted to the nuclear arms race if, as I believe will be true and most gratefully so, they have never even been used. From the perspective of the twenty-first century, it may well be that this waste will emerge as the primary evil we will have suffered from nuclear weaponry, rather than the nuclear holocaust which appears at present as such a clear and pressing danger.

I have a similar feeling about the severe international tensions between the portion of the world dominated by ideas of private capital, free enterprise, and democratic government, and the other part of the world dominated by ideas of the supremacy of labor over capital in the economic order, the dominance of the proletariat, and regimentation in government. This capitalist-communist confrontation has certainly played the leading role in defining the moral imperatives for peace for the last thirty years. It seems to me inevitable that this role must steadily wane during the next thirty years.

The ideas of Marx and Lenin on the one hand, and of laissez-faire capitalism on the other, had a central relevance for the stage which the industrial revolution had reached in the latter part of the nineteenth century and the early part of the twentieth. At its present stage late in the twentieth century, however, neither set of ideas has any relevance to the actual way in which the economy operates in either capitalist or communist countries. The transformation which has taken place in all major industries and financial institutions, to computers, automated processes, systems analysis and control, and the high level of technical skill required of all workers, has resulted in a structure in which both questions of the ownership of property and the exploitation of labor by owners no longer have any meaning. It would make no detectable difference in the management or operation of General Motors if all of the stock in the corporation presently owned by a very large and effectively anonymous group of stockholders were distributed among all citizens in proportion, say, to the income tax paid by each. The equivalent of General Motors, International Telephone and Telegraph and DuPont operate the same way with the same kind of managers and technical specialists in the Soviet Union or Yugoslavia as they do in the United States or France. In all capitalist countries the labor force through its unions and strike capability plays an even more determinative role in the total economy than does its counterpart in communist countries. On the other hand, experience to date in communist countries certainly bears out the superiority of private ownership and operation of small service businesses such as filling stations, motels, and the like.

During the remainder of this century, the irrelevance of both capital and labor to the actual problems of the production of goods and services will become increasingly evident. The very ideas of the ownership of the means of production and of a proletariat class simply do not arise on a spaceship. As we crowd together on the planet and fill and subdue it, the earth is becoming more and more our spaceship. The limited character of its remaining resources will, as we have seen, become increasingly determinative for both capitalist and communist economies. For both of them the problems of sharing in the utilization of the earth's Commons and reorienting their economies from a condition of affluence based on continuously improving economic development and increasing Gross National Product, to a condition of scarcity based on priority utilization and conservation of scarce but essential materials will increasingly dominate all national concerns. The moral imperatives previously directed toward securing the coexistence of capitalist and communist ideologies will correspondingly become redirected toward a resolution of the moral dilemmas of the Commons and of the joint access of all nations to increasingly scarce reserves of essential resources. If warfare is to be avoided and peace maintained for the remainder of this century, these are the moral imperatives which must increasingly command our best thought and action.

The next thirty years of this century is to be a time of judgment for the human species on this planet. Like the sixth century B.C. for Israel or the fifth century A.D. for Rome, it will be a period of agonizing readjustments when everything in which we have previously found stability and security crumbles about us, and the new order which will finally emerge from the destruction of the old is only dimly discernible. As we crowd together on the planet, old bitternesses of race and tribe and nation will become increasingly exacerbated. We no doubt face social paroxysms of an intensity greater than any we have so far experienced. If warfare does break out over any of the old issues, it will be doubly tragic, since these issues are all dying in any event. It is, therefore, especially tragic to base our moral imperatives for peace on the categories of the sixties. All of us—Soviets, Mainland Chinese, and Americans; Thais and Cambodians; Israelis and Arabs—face in common the reality of the same judgment upon us all and the same new imperatives for our future joint habitation of our common spaceship earth. It behooves us all to recognize the common threat to our successfully doing so which we all face in the same way. If we can do this, we will all come to see that the issues which now dominate our thinking and threaten our peace are dying or already dead. The moral issues of real significance for making peacefully the transition to the new order which all must accomplish in the remainder of this century arise out of the planetary imperatives of the earth's Commons and her scarce resources as we take her over as our spaceship.

Notes

CHAPTER III: THE DRIVE TO POWER

1. Adolphe Cournot, *Traité de l'enchaînement des idées fondamentales dans les sciences et dans l'histoire* (Paris, 1861), p. 461.

2. This is an ordinance dated August 1749, due to d'Aguesseau. [Henri Francois d'Aguesseau (1668-1751), French jurist, Chancellor of France 1717-18, 1720-22, 1737-50.] A suggestion was recently made in the U.S. Senate that after forty years the assets of foundations should be dispersed.

3. Adam Smith, *Wealth of Nations,* Book V, chap. 1.

4. John Ramsey McCulloch, *Dictionary of Commerce and Commercial Navigation,* 1834 ed., p. 377.

5. See Aristotle, *The Constitution of Athens,* Book II, F. G. Kenyon, ed. (London, 1895).

6. Alan T. Peacock and Jack Wiseman, *The Growth of Public Expenditure in the United Kingdom* (London, National Bureau of Economic Research, 1961), pp. 42, 55.

7. Moses Abramovitz and Vera Eliasberg, *The Growth of Public Employment in Great Britain* (New York: National Bureau of Economic Research, 1957), p. 25.

8. Edmund Burke, *Letters on a Regicide Peace.*

9. Elie Halévy's communication to the Société Française de Philosophie, 28 November 1936, published in his posthumously collected essays, *L'Ere des tyrannies* (Paris, Gallimard, 1938).

10. Published only in Blanc's newspaper *Le Nouveau Monde,* it deserves republication.

11. Margaret Cole, ed., *The Webbs and Their Work* (London, 1949), p. 6.

12. Emile Faguet, "Le Socialisme en 1899," in *Questions politiques* (Paris, 1899), and *Le Socialisme en 1907* (Paris, 1907).

13. B. Mirkine-Guetzévitch, *Les Constitutions de l'Europe nouvelle* (Paris, 1929), p. 22.

CHAPTER IV: MAN'S NATURAL DESIRE FOR PEACE

1. Edward P. Cheyney, "Law in History," *American Historical Review*, XXIX, 2 (Jan. 1924), pp. 231-48.

2. J. B. Bury, *The Idea of Progress* (New York: Macmillan, 1932).

3. *New York Times*, Mar. 12, 1969, section K.

4. Herbert V. Guenther, *Tibetan Buddhism Without Mystification: The Buddhist Way from Original Tibetan Sources* (Leiden: E. J. Brill, 1966). For a review see *Journal of Asian Studies*, XXVII, 1 (Nov. 1967), 156-8. Guenther is also the author of *Life and Teaching of Naropa* (Oxford: Clarendon Press, 1963), and *Yuganaddha: The Tantric View of Life* (Banaras, 1952).

5. Guenther, *Tibetan Buddhism*, pp. 4-5. Guenther finds six forms of life recognized in Buddhism: denizens of hell, spirits, animals, men, demons, and gods. Of these, only animals and men are physically in existence. The lower three are man's brute forms, and the latter two the outgrowth of overreaching himself. Animals operate by appetite, men by mind.

6. José Ortega y Gasset, *Toward a Philosophy of History* (New York: W. W. Norton, 1941), pp. 217, 220.

7. Guenther, *Tibetan Buddhism*, pp. 3, 17, 48-9.

8. See Martin Buber, *I and Thou*, trans. Ronald Gregor Smith (Edinburgh: T & T Clark, 1937), espec. pp. vi-vii, 3-5, 8-9.

   For Kant's categories see Immanuel Kant, *Critique of Pure Reason,,* trans. Norman Kemp Smith (New York: St. Martin's Press, 1965; originally published by Macmillan, 1929), pt. I, 1, 2, pp. 111-19; and Paul Edwards, ed., *Encyclopedia of Philosophy* (New York: Macmillan, 1967), V, p. 59.

   Marx discusses this matter in *Capital* (New York: International Publishers, 1967), I, p. I, chap. 1, section 4, pp. 71-83. ("The Fetishism of Commodities and the Secret Thereof.") See also Lloyd D. Easton and Kurt H. Guddat, *Writings of the Young Marx on Philosophy and Society* (New York: Doubleday, 1967), pp. 309-10, 414-15.

9. Guenther, *Tibetan Buddhism*, pp. 18-19.

10. *Ibid.*, pp. 18, 42.

11. *Ibid.*, p. 19.

12. *Ibid.*, pp. 49-50.

13. Bergen Evans makes a delightful comment on leaders in his *The Spoor of*

Spooks and Other Nonsense (New York: Alfred A. Knopf, 1954), p. 75. He says: "Entrance blanks always ask if the applicant is a 'leader' or a 'follower,' and leave no doubt that the former is desirable. It may be doubted, however, that it is. There is no necessary connection between the desire to lead and the ability to lead somewhere that will be to the advantage of those led. 'A craving for public attention,' as has been pointed out, 'is not in any sense a qualification for public responsibility.' Leadership is more likely to be assumed by the aggressive than the able, and those who scramble to the top are more often motivated by their own inner torments than by any demand for their guidance."

14. James Legge, *The Four Books* (New York: Paragon Book Corp., 1966 reprint of 1923 Shanghai ed., "The Doctrine of the Mean" (Chung Yung 中庸), I, 4-5, pp. 351-52.

15. *Ibid.*, "Confucian Analects" (Lu Yü 論語), II, chap. 14, p. 18. Waley translates this as follows: "A gentleman can see a question from all sides without bias. The small man is biased and can see a question only from one side." Arthur Waley, trans., *The Analects of Confucius* (London: George Allen and Unwin, 1938; reprinted as Vintage Book V-173 by Alfred A. Knopf and Random House, New York), p. 91. The key characters are 君子周而不比. The "rolled up universe" consists of six directions, zenith, nadir, and four cardinal points, "rolled together." Hence 六合卷 Legge, *Four Books*, p. 348.

16. Legge, *Four Books*, "The Doctrine of the Mean," XIII, 1, p. 364.

17. *Ibid.*, 3, p. 365.

18. *Ibid.*, XX, 18 et seq., from p. 394, espec. XXV, 3, p. 403. The key characters are 誠 (sincerity); and 合外内 (union of internal and external).

19. *Ibid.*, XXVII, 6, p. 409 et seq. The key character is 德 .

20. Legge, *Four Books*, "Confucian Analects," II, chap. 3, pt. 1, p. 13; cf. Waley, *Analects*, II, 3, p. 88.

21. Legge, *Four Books*, "Confucian Analects," XVI, chap. 1, pt. 10, p. 240; cf. Waley, *Analects*, XVI, 10, p. 203.

22. Legge, *Four Books*, "Confucian Analects," XII, chap. 19, p. 168; cf. Waley, *Analects*, XII, 19, p. 168.

23. Legge, *Four Books*, "The Great Learning" (Ta Hsüeh 大學), espec. par. 5, p. 313. Note the progression in the characters 物格 to 知 plus 誠 brings 天下平 (investigate things-knowledge-sincerity-peace). The last three characters are translated by Legge

as "tranquility," but the literal meaning is Under Heaven, or Everywhere Under Heaven, Peace.

24. Wm. T. deBary, *Sources of Chinese Tradition* (New York: Columbia University Press, 1960),"Taoism," chap. 4, pp. 50-87. Wu-wei 無 為 .

25. See Immanuel Kant, *Perpetual Peace*, with a preface by Nicholas Murray Butler (Los Angeles: U.S. Library Assoc., Inc., 1932). Originally published as *Zum ewigen Frieden* in 1795; this text follows the first edition translated from the German and published in London in 1896. Kant argues that though "war appears ingrafted" in men "as they compose a class of animals" nature leads man "without prejudice to his liberty" toward "practical reason" whereby "endowed with understanding" he will seek and find "perpetual peace." This is very like the Buddhist argument, except that Kant, perhaps naively, does not regard individual "moral reform" as necessary. Rather, "It only demands that one should desire advantage from the mechanism of nature, in order so to direct the opposition of personal interests, that all the individuals who compose a nation should constrain one another to range themselves beneath a coercive power of legislation, and thus introduce a pacific state of legislation." Pp. 44-6.

26. Plato, *The Republic*, pt. II, appendix.

27. *Ibid.*, chap. 9.

28. *Ibid.*, I, chap. 2-3.

29. Albert Camus, *Les Justes*, including his postscript, "Les Pharisiens de la Justice," in Germaine Brée, ed., *Albert Camus* (New York: Dell, Pub. Co., 1963). Cf. *Les Justes, piéces en cinq actes* (Paris: Gallimard, 1950).

30. Tibetan Buddhism would add that the perpetrators of injustice also are innocents, being men in their inferior nature.

31. Albert Camus, *L'Etat de* siége *: spectacle en trois parties* (Paris: Gallimard, 1948). This work also appears in Camus's *Caligula and Three Other Plays*, trans. Stuart Gilbert (New York: Alfred A. Knopf, 1958); Albert Camus, *La Peste* (Paris: Gallimard, 1947), also pub. in Paris by Librairie Larousse in 1948, and trans. by Stuart Gilbert (New York: Alfred A. Knopf, 1948).

32. Georg Wilhelm Friedrich Hegel, *The Philosophy of History*, trans. J. Sibree (New York: Dover Publications, 1956), espec. introduction, sections 1 and 3, and pt. IV ("The German World"), section 3 ("The Modern Time"); T. M. Knox, trans., *Hegel's Philosophy of the Right* (London: Oxford University Press, 1967), espec. the preface and pt. III, subsection 3 ("The State"). Perhaps Mussolini even more than Hitler articulated the extension to absurdity of Hegelian statism. He said, "The Fascist conception of the state is all-embracing; outside of it no human or cultural values can exist, much less have value. Thus understood, Fascism is totalitarian, and the Fascist state—a synthesis and a unit inclusive of all values—interprets, develops, and

potentiates the whole life of a people." Quoted in Alan Cassels, *Fascist Italy* (New York: Thomas Y. Crowell, 1968), p. 69.

33. Shlomo Avineri, *The Social and Political Thought of Karl Marx* (Cambridge: At the University Press, 1968), espec. chap. on "The French Revolution and The Terror," pp. 185-98; cf. Shlomo Avineri, ed., *Karl Marx on Colonialism and Modernizaton: His Dispatches and Other Writings on China, India, Mexico, The Middle East, and North Africa* (Garden City, N.Y.: Doubleday, 1968).

34. Woodrow Wilson is reputed to have told a gathering of Princeton students: "We are not put into this world to sit still and know; we are put in it to act." Gamaliel Bradford, "Brains Win and Lose: Woodrow Wilson," in *The Quick and the Dead,* Boston: Houghton Mifflin, 1931), p. 66. Unfortunately, Wilson was merely a "mediocre man" by Buddhist standards.

35. Donald Swearer, "The Relation Between Knowledge and Meditation in Early Buddhism": lecture delivered at the University of Pennsylvania, November 14, 1968.

36. The imagery of searching out scorpions in the house is used by Guenther, *Tibetan Buddhism*, p. 114.

37. Tsong-kha-pa, "The Three Principal Aspects of the Path of the Buddha," trans. Jeffrey Hopkins, unpublished, pp. 14-18. The transferring of love from mother to worst enemy results in the development of a "mind of equality" toward all human beings. I am indebted to my son Fran, who is a Danforth Fellow in Philosophy at the Yale Graduate School, for bringing this and some of the other philosophical materials used in this paper to my attention.

38. Berenice Carroll, "The Historian and the Dilemma," in Charles A. Barker, ed., *Power and Law: The American Dilemma in World Relations* (to be published by Johns Hopkins Press), conclusion.

39. "Communication," *American Historical Review*, LXII, 4 (July 1957), pp. 1055-57.

40. The Japanese educator Fukuzawa Yukichi employed a charming term, *uji-mushi* (worms and bugs) principle, to get across this idea. *Uji-mushi* literally means "worms and bugs" but it is also a Japanese slang term for children, like "kids" or "small fry." In working out our problems, said Fukuzawa, we should never forget that our activities are like the play of children, and our institutions are the product of such "child's play." If we take them too seriously we fall into "indulgence in the ostentation of institutions." Maruyama Masao, "Tukuzawa Yukichi no Tetsugaku" (The Philosophy of Fukuzawa Yukichi), *Kokka Gakkai Zasshi*, LXI, 3 (1947), pp. 129-63. Cf. F. Hilary Conroy, *The Japanese Seizure of Korea* (Philadelphia: Univ. of Penn. Press, 1960), pp. 130-32.

156

41. Johan Huizinga, *Homo Ludens: A Study of the Play Element in Culture* (Boston: Beacon Press, 1955). See especially Huizinga's captivating discourses on the "nature and significance of play" (chap. 1) and "play and contest as civilizing functions" (chap. 3). In *Praise of Folly*, written in 1509, Disiderius Erasmus plays delightfully on this theme (see the Oxford edition, 1913).

42. Loren C. Eiseley gives a succinct argument on this point, while reviewing the disagreement with Darwin of his contemporary, Alfred Russel Wallace, in "Was Darwin Wrong about the Human Brain?" *Harper's Magazine*, November 1955, pp. 66-70. Lewis Mumford stresses the same theme in "Speculations on Prehistory," *American Scholar*, Winter, 1966-7, pp. 43-53. Addison H. Leitch presents an interesting question in his article entitled "Evolution As an Easygoing Theory," *Pacific Philosophy Forum*, VI, 3 (February 1968), pp. 69-78. Noting that evolution in nature results in "degeneration" (e.g., a plot left untended goes to weeds), he asks why then should there be an upward movement via lower animals to man, concluding that the evolution theory glosses such matters over too easily to be scientifically valid. In a recent discourse on "The Biological Constraints of Homo Sapiens," René Dubos put forth the interesting proposition that whatever evolutionary changes may have occurred in previous types of man, Homo sapiens has not changed biologically for at least 50,000 years. And the range of variation between early and modern man is no greater than among modern men. Thus, he said, "a Cro-Magnon man could certainly function in an IBM plant and with luck might become president of the company." Danforth Foundation Lecture, delivered at Buck Hill Falls, Pa., December 5, 1969.

43. Recently there has been a spate of attractively written pieces on "natural" aggressive instincts of fish, birds, animals, insects, and by indirection at least, man. Cf. Robert Andraey, *African Genesis* (New York: Atheneum, 1963), and *The Territorial Imperative* (Kingsport Press, 1966); Konrad Lorenz, *Man Meets Dog*, trans. Marjorie Kerr Wilson (Baltimore: Penguin Books, 1964); *King Solomon's Ring: New Light on Animal Ways* (New York: Harcourt, Brace and World, 1966); Desmond Morris, *The Naked Ape: A Zoologist's Study of the Human Animal* (New York: McGraw-Hill, 1967). However, it should be observed that Lorenz, at least, specifically notes an "appeasement" phenomenon which precludes a fight to the death in many species, and that he concludes with an avowal of "optimism" on man's ability to work out his aggressions through sports and other nondestructive behavior. *On Aggression*, pp. 132-38, 275-99. Ashley Montagu, reviewing these books, says that with so much aggression there would be "no men left, if only this [aggression] were going on," and he concludes that the problem lies "not in nature but in nurture." Ashley Montagu, 'Original Sin': Redivivus," *Journal of Historical Studies*, II, 2 (Spring, 1969), pp. 132-55.

44. Conway Zirkle, "Darwin's Impact upon Modern Thought," in *The Cultural Heritage of 20th Century Man* (Philadelphia: Penn. Literary Review and The Philomathean Society, 1955), pp. 63-71.

45. See Segawa Yoshinobu, "Hawaii Imin Mondai" (The Problem of Japanese Immigration to Hawaii) (Pt. 1), *Kokusaihō Gaikō Zasshi*, LXVI, 1 (June 1967), section 6 on "The Problem of Voting Rights." Cf. F. Hilary Conroy, *The Japanese Frontier in Hawaii, 1868-1898* (Berkeley: University of California Press, 1953), pp. 97-99. A particularly interesting letter, which gives most of Austin's arguments, is Austin to Ando, October 17, 1888, printed in Japanese Foreign Office, *Nihon Gaiko Bunsho* (Japanese Foreign Affairs Documents), XXI, pp. 461-64. See also Merze Tate, *Hawaii: Reciprocity or Annexation* (East Lansing: Michigan State University Press, 1968), pp. 197-210, and her *The United States and the Hawaiian Kingdom* (New Haven: Yale University Press, 1965), pp. 60-110, 318, for background on these matters.

46. Ralph S. Kuykendall and A. Grove Day, *Hawaii: A History* (New York: Prentice-Hall, 1948), pp. 170-72. The career of Gibson is the subject of a vignette essay in James A. Michener and A. Grove Day, *Rascals in Paradise* (New York: Random House, 1957).

47. Legge, *Four Books*, "Confucian Analects," I, chap. 2:2, p. 3. The character for "radical" is   (a tree with a root). It also means root, source, and books.

CHAPTER VI:
TECHNOLOGY AND PEACE: THE ROLE OF BIOLOGICAL RESEARCH

1. They also constituted my testimony before the Subcommittee on National Security Policy and Scientific Developments, of the House Committe on Foreign Affairs, Rep. Clement J. Zablocki, Chairman, December 2, 1969, 91st Congress, First Session. These hearings offer an informative overview of U.S. policy on biological and chemical warfare.

2. See Appendix I at the conclusion of this essay for text of the President's statement.

3. Unilateral renunciation of biological warfare capability was a step much beyond what I had advocated. In the light of Soviet recalcitrance, it may seem to have weakened our bargaining position for the short term. However, the self-imposed moratorium is not irrevocable, and surely would not be sustained in the face of evidence of tangible abuse of its intent by a potential adversary.

CHAPTER IX: IDEOLOGIES OF VIOLENCE AND SOCIAL CHANGE

1. H. L. Nieberg, "The Uses of Violence," *Journal of Conflict Resolution*, vol. 7, no. 1 (1963), p. 43.

2. William H. Grier and Price N. Cobb, *The Politics of Protest*, Jerome H. Skolnick, ed., (New York: Simon and Schuster, Inc., 1969).

158

3. *Ibid*. p. xi.

4. Disregard of these considerations is only one of the gross failings in the scandalous piece of propaganda for violence which appears under the auspices of the National Commission on the Causes and Prevention of Violence, *The Politics of Protest* edited by Skolnick. It is a report of one of the Commission's Task Forces. Professor Milton R. Konvitz of Cornell University, one of America's great civil libertarians, outstanding for his scholarship, compassion, and scrupulous sense of fairness, writes of Skolnick's report: "The main thrust of the book, however, is to validate political violence in America. There is very little in the body of the work that would tend to dispel the myth of violent progress, and that would make 'the values of a constitutional democracy' credible, not in some utopian society but in the United States." *Saturday Review*, LII, 46 (November 15, 1969), pp. 42-43.

5. Nieberg, "Uses of Violence," *loc. cit.*

CHAPTER X: A CLIMATE FOR CHANGE

1. Sydney C. Roberts, *Introduction to Cambridge* (Cambridge: University Press, 1934), p. 2.

2. Abrams vs. the United States, vol. 250, U.S. 616,630 (1919).

3. From *The Poetry of Robert Frost* edited by Edward Connery Lathem. Copyright 1916, (c) 1969 by Holt, Rinehart and Winston, Inc. Copyright 1944 by Robert Frost. Reprinted by permission of Holt, Rinehart and Winston, Inc.